W9-BNH-368

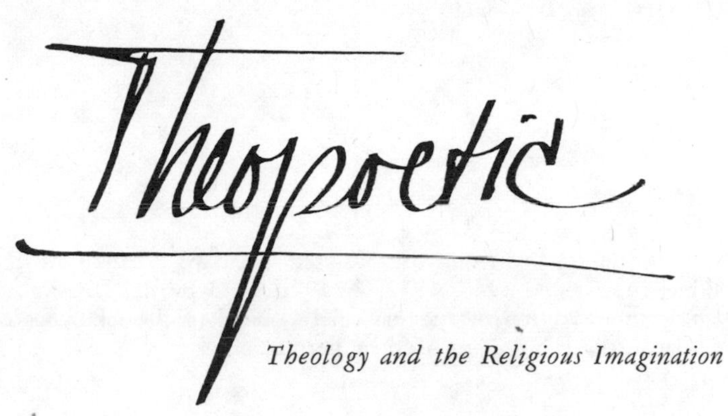

Theology and the Religious Imagination

by

Amos Niven Wilder

Fortress Press

Philadelphia

Biblical quotations from the Revised Standard Version of the Bible, copyrighted 1946, 1952, © 1971, 1973 by the Division of Christian Education of the National Council of the Churches of Christ in the U.S.A., are used by permission.

The lines from "East Coker" and from "The Dry Salvages" by T. S. Eliot are from his *Four Quartets,* copyright © 1943 by Harcourt Brace Jovanovich, Inc., and are used by permission.
The lines from "Starlight Like Intuition Pierced the Twelve" by Delmore Schwartz are from his *Selected Poems: Summer Knowledge*, copyright © 1950 by New Directions Publishing Corporation, and are used by permission.
The lines from "The Dishonest Mailman" by Robert Creeley are from his *For Love*, copyright © 1962 by Robert Creeley, and are used by permission of Charles Scribner's Sons.

Library of Congress Catalog Card Number 75-36458
ISBN 0-8006-0435-0

5414K75 Printed in U.S.A. 1-435

Contents

Foreword

For the focus and themes of this book I am specially indebted to a number of friends and discussions. The initial chapter goes back to a short talk I was asked to give in the spring of 1972. The occasion was the presentation to me of a volume of essays edited by Howard E. Hunter and entitled *The Humanities, Religion and the Arts Tomorrow*.[1] I chose the topic "Theology and Theopoetic," and a short discussion followed. I believe that I had picked up the terms "theopoetic" and "theopoesis" from Stanley Hopper and his students, no doubt in one or another of the remarkable consultations on hermeneutics and language which he had organized at Drew and Syracuse to which so many of us are indebted.

I take this occasion to register my thanks to the editor and to the other contributors to that volume. Some of them were able to be present at the little ceremony; besides the editor, Harvey Cox, Robert Steele, Walter Wagoner, Jane and John Dillenberger who collaborated on a joint contribution as did Dorothy Austin and Roger Hazelton, were also present. The other contributors, not able to be present, were Nathan A. Scott, Jr., Charles W. Kegley, Tom F. Driver, Charles Stoneburner, John W. Dixon, Jr., and Stanley R. Hopper. I thank them all for

1. Howard E. Hunter, *The Humanities, Religion and the Arts Tomorrow* (New York: Holt, Rinehart and Winston, 1972).

their participation in this offering. Their names well suggest the promising frontiers and tasks of the religious imagination in our time. The present book is indebted in many ways to their papers.

On the same occasion a small collection of poems, *Of Alphus*, with a silk-screen cover, was presented to me—poems written by members of the Harvard Divinity School community, the first of a series. The title is derived from the medieval epigraph on the title page:

No egg on Friday Alph will eat,
  but drunken he will be on Friday still.
O what a pure religious man is he.

Since the epigraph and the dedication to myself appear on that same title page there is some ambiguity as to the identity of the "drunken" Alph. It is to be hoped that the imputation can be turned if it be supposed, as Ephesians 5:18 suggests, that Alph is not "drunk with wine" but "filled with the Spirit," or at least with the Muse.

Many of the poets represented in this collection had been members of a Colloquium on Religion and Literature of which I had been the faculty consultant during the spring semester. I take this opportunity to thank David M. Robinson, who had initiated the colloquium, as well as Paul Holbrook, Travis du Priest, Michael Masopust, Gene Arnould, and Eugene Krause, who with others shared in our discussions and in the publication.

The present writing owes much to one larger circle. Participation in the committees, symposia, and wine-cellar discussions of the Society for the Arts, Religion, and Contemporary Culture (ARC) during these recent years has provided much stimulus, orientation, and content, as will be seen in various references in the text.[2] Special acknowledgment is due here to our Executive Secretary, Mrs. Eugene Meyer, and to our most recent presidents, Stanley Hopper and Emery Valyi.

The Christian Century Foundation graciously granted permission to reprint my articles from *The Christian Century* entitled "Theology and Theopoetic," nos. 1, 2, and 3, published as follows: "Theology and Theopoetic," vol. 90, no. 21 (23 May 1973); "The Renewal of the Religious Imagination," vol. 90, no. 44 (5 December 1973); "Ecstacy, Imagination and Insight," vol. 91, no. 10 (13 March 1974); these articles, in revised and extended form, appear here as chapters 1, 4, and 5. *The Journal of Religious Thought* allowed the inclusion of my article, "Contemporary Mythologies and Theological Renewal," published in vol. 27, no. 3 (Autumn-Winter 1970), pp. 5–12, which appears here, in extended form, in chapter 3.

2. Specially relevant here are certain publications sponsored by ARC or growing out of its activities: (1) *Myths, Dreams and Religion,* ed. Joseph Campbell (New York: Dutton, 1970); (2) my own Tillich Lectures with other of my papers in *The New Voice: Religion, Literature, Hermeneutics* (New York: Herder, 1969) (out of print); (3) *The Grotesque in Contemporary Art and Literature,* ed. James Luther Adams (forthcoming); (4) *Imagination, Meaning and the Creative Act,* ed. Stanley R. Hopper (forthcoming). See also the files of the Society's Bulletin, *ARC Directions,* nos. 1–7 (1966–70) with contributions by Frederick Franck, Robert Sowers, Rollo May, Wolfgang Zucker, Samuel H. Miller, Joseph Campbell, Alan Watts, Meyer Schapiro, Jane Dillenberger, and others.

1

Theology and Theopoetic

It is in the area of liturgics—the idiom and metaphors of prayer and witness—that the main impasse lies today for the Christian.

It is at the level of the imagination that the fateful issues of our new world-experience must first be mastered. It is here that culture and history are broken, and here that the church is polarized. Old words do not reach across the new gulfs, and it is only in vision and oracle that we can chart the unknown and new-name the creatures.

Before the message there must be the vision, before the sermon the hymn, before the prose the poem.

Before any new theologies however secular and radical there must be a contemporary theopoetic. The structures of faith and confession have always rested on hierophanies and images. But in each new age and climate the theopoetic of the church is reshaped in inseparable relation to the general imagination of the time.[1]

These theses written to introduce a recent collection of verse have a direct bearing not only on liturgics but on all religious language today including theology itself. Religious communication generally must overcome a long addiction to the discursive, the rationalistic, and the prosaic. And the Christian imagination must go halfway to meet the new dreams, mystiques, and mythologies that are gestating in our time.

1. From the Foreword to *Grace Confounding: Poems* by Amos N. Wilder (Philadelphia: Fortress Press, 1972), p. ix.

My plea for a theopoetic means doing more justice to the role of the symbolic and the prerational in the way we deal with experience. We should recognize that human nature and human societies are more deeply motivated by images and fabulations than by ideas. This is where power lies and the future is shaped.

This plea therefore means according a greater role to the imagination in all aspects of the religious life. But "imagination" here should not be taken in an insipid sense. Imagination is a necessary component of all profound knowing and celebration; all remembering, realizing, and anticipating; all faith, hope, and love. When imagination fails doctrines become ossified, witness and proclamation wooden, doxologies and litanies empty, consolations hollow, and ethics legalistic.

It is at the level of the imagination that any full engagement with life takes place. It is not enough for the church to be on guard against the Philistine in the world. Philistinism invades Christianity from within wherever the creative and mythopoetic dimension of faith is forfeited. When this happens doctrine becomes a caricature of itself. Then that which once gave life begins to lull and finally to suffocate us.

I

To make good this plea I must first obviate a number of objections and misunderstandings.

1) This emphasis should not be disparaged, as it often is, as a plea for a shallow aestheticism. With our moralistic and rationalist mind-set it is too easy to shelve any appeal for the rights of the imagination as a matter of "mere poetry." But what is in question here is not an irresponsible aestheticism but the essential dynamics of the heart and soul .

2) It is not here implied that imagery and ritual are more crucial than Christian love and action. But significant action needs to be oriented and empowered by a true vision and meaningful celebration.

3) It is no answer when the churchman points to the large place of religious imagery and symbolism in the actual piety and observance of the churches. Certainly the hymn book, the prayers, and the sermon evoke the dramatic archetypes of the faith just as do the rites and customs associated with Christmas and Easter. But what we have here too often is religious sentiment rather than exorcism, nostalgia rather than actualized revelation. The true mythos of Christianity does not come to life, partly because as stereotype it is not free to generate its own contemporary communication, and partly because it is not brought into costly relation with our current fates and choices.

4) It is not my intention to disallow the necessary task of rigorous thinking about the faith and critical study of its sources which we call theology. With many others today, however, I would like to see the horizons, agenda, methods, and so the very givens of theology enriched. On this point I should add the following considerations.

Though theology strictly understood is an intellectual if not a discursive activity yet the work of the greatest theologians has always been shot through with the imagination. The kind of truth and reason that theology is concerned to clarify does not permit of merely abstract, wooden, or pedantic treatment. Witness the procedure of Augustine, Calvin, or Jonathan Edwards.

When I speak of the need for a richer agenda I can illustrate by what is called "cosmic theology." There is no realm of experience in which even recent dogmatics has been more anachronistic than that of nature. Development of the natural sciences including astronomy together with space exploration has effected as radical a revolution in our outlook and sensibility as that which overcame the Ptolemaic universe

But this new sensibility is also evident in the arts with their heightened awareness of the elements of perception, the wonder of what is immediately presented to consciousness in touch, sight, and sound. Reality has become dizzying and uncharted but every particular contact with it all the more fresh and unpredictable. Thus the revolution in cosmology has shocked not only our intellectual but also our imaginative categories. As has been recognized, the resulting surprise and insecurity is reflected variously in the order of phantasy, space fiction, astrology, the apocalyptic imagination, and ecological mystiques.

But the mythical cosmology of Scripture and the Christian view of nature—when freed from distortions and impoverishments incident to a long history—have the resources to welcome and order all such new imaginative transactions with our theater of existence. "Cosmic theology" takes hold of certain extramundane, mythical perspectives as found, for example, in the Epistles to the Colossians and the Ephesians, in a way which answers to the new categories of our modern vision of the creation. If Lucretius as a poet of nature's mysteries has his modern counterpart in a poet like Perse, so a theologian like Joseph Sittler today contemporizes for us the cosmic perspectives of some of the early church fathers. Even in the case of St. Paul we are today freeing ourselves from the narrow anthropological focus in which his outlook has been obscured as we learn to appreciate the cosmic sense of his doctrine of justification.

The view of nature in the Old Testament and in the teachings of Jesus, as in the Canticles of St. Francis, is congenial to the contemporary reverence for our natural habitat as it is widely rediscovered. It is important that these things should be clarified in a period concerned with ecology when older cultural sanctions for the exploitation of nature have been so widely misunderstood. But it is only at the level of a theopoetic that these contemporary issues can be rightly explored. We can learn more from the Psalms and the Book of Job about man's relation to the earth and the creatures as the Bible teaches than by some polemic twisting of a verse in Genesis.

When, on the other hand, I speak of the need today for an enrichment of the methods of theology I can illustrate by the contribution afforded from the side of secular literary criticism. Biblical theology and interpretation have of late taken on new vitality as we have learned to read the biblical texts with the tools and approaches employed by our colleagues specialized in literary studies. This kind of enrichment has been particularly evident in all that concerns the appreciation of plastic language and poetic styles. More recently illumination of matters of basic import has resulted from attention to aspects of genre and structure. More generally, wide scrutiny today of the relation of religion and the arts has opened up the deeper dynamics of communication and meaning.

5) Finally, one further caveat should be mentioned. Before we join the chorus of those who repeat that the renewal of Christianity is a matter of the renewal of its language we should recognize how difficult this is. It is a costly transaction and cannot be manipulated.

We hear a good deal today in secular and academic quarters about the arts and strategies of communication. The implication often is that by substituting a short word for a long one, or a colloquial term for one more dated, or a topical allusion or illustration for one drawn from an older context, we can "get across" our meaning or appeal. This may have its validity for advertizing or some kinds of popularization. Former president Melancthon M. Stryker of Hamilton College, a noted preacher in the old style, once wrote an essay in words of one syllable in praise of "the stroke of quick speech, sharp of blade and sure of hilt." It is of interest to learn that this essay is now again circulating, having been recently cited "in a newsletter for those in the internal communication field."

But all such recipes and programmed strategies fall short of accounting for the full mystery of language where deep calls to deep. The textbooks of rhetoric provide only an outside equipment. Any fresh renewal of language or rebirth of images arises from within and from beyond our control. Nevertheless we can help prepare the event, both by moral and spiritual discipline and by attention to the modes and vehicles of the Word. Of first importance here are the deeper vocabulary and idiom of the Spirit, and all that is suggested by such terms as primordial language and dynamic symbol.

II

Two aspects of my plea can be distinguished. One can be called the intramural and one the extramural, though the two are closely related. The extramural consideration arises out of the many evidences in our culture of a turn toward what we can speak of loosely as the mystical, the prerational, and the imaginative. This is not only a matter of the "counter-culture" but also of the modern arts and even of the most sophisticated philosophy. The more our scientific technoculture ripens the more it seems to call forth, as a kind of shadow, a mentality compounded of magic and mythology. But this new climate reminds the church of its own deeper dream and here we have the intramural aspect. What forms will a theopoetic take today which will both quicken the tradition and at the same time speak to the general imagination of the age?

In an age which in other respects exhibits a rebirth of phantasy and the surreal—a revolt against the "objective consciousness"—why should the language of faith be so largely confined to the discursive mode or to stereotypes that have forfeited their explosive power? The counter-culture today follows a true instinct in exploring even dubious versions of ecstasy and phantasy in the absence of more authentic ones.

Yet when the wells of natural impulse are so blocked and the water level of instinctive spontaneity is so low as in the spiritual terrain of today why should so many feel that they have to resort to deceitful springs and exotic oracles, to dowsing with hazel wands and to divinations and astrology, to elixirs and mirages? Jeremiah long ago contrasted "broken cisterns that can hold no water" with "the fountain of living waters."

If we hear today precisely in some theological circles of a dancing god, of a harlequin Christ, and of the motifs of play and the playing child and the clown-saint, we should recognize the hunger for innocence and naiveté so attested. They are a protest against the penury of the Spirit which ever recurs when valid older dramas and fabulations no longer resonate.

A creative theopoetic is called for, therefore, not only to vitalize a traditional theology but also to relate our Christian experience to the new sensibility of our time and its images and cults. In the modern arts, in the media, in various subcultures we see not only iconoclasm and revolt but also new structures of the imagination taking shape. Here our new sense of reality, both cosmic and psychological, finds its symbolic expression both in art and in life-style. Any traditional religion must come to terms with these developments.

III

I turn to the intramural aspect of my plea. Any renewal of Christian discourse and liturgy today will be the work of the Spirit and therefore involve those dramatic categories and poetics which are alone adequate to the issues at stake. Here no doubt the classic symbols of faith emerge again in power, but only as mediated through our modern apperception.

The church today has widely lost and all but forgotten the experience of glory which lies at the heart of Christianity. Indeed, in one form or another that experience is a main trait of all religion just because human nature and existence itself derive from inexhaustible energies and cataracts of light and life. That the original plenitude is so widely smothered in the creaturely condition only enforces the special and irreplaceable role of religion in witnessing to it.

Yet how can theology or piety give any account of faith so understood without a continual rehearsal of visionary representations, dramatic vehicles, and affectional language? When Paul writes about interpreting "spirituals" (*pneumatika*), or "the things which are freely given to us by God" in "*spiritual language*," this is part of what he means. He certainly does not mean wan and bloodless abstractions. Witness the mythopoetic scenarios and sensuous tropes which undergird his instruction and encouragement. And what is also to the point in our present discussion is that this depth-language of Paul chimed with the scenarios and quests of his Hellenistic readers.

As in Paul's day so today the intramural and the extramural aspects of a valid theopoetic merge with each other.

When the Gospel breaks through the impasse in the household of faith, at the same time it speaks to the questing of our contemporaries. At no point is this clearer than as regards the inarticulate hunger for plenitude, for transcendence, even for ecstasy both within and without the religious institutions. If the category of glory in the faith and worship of the church were more adequately evoked—that is, in ways that chimed with the modern man's self-picture and world-picture—then these hungers could be more fully met than they are at present either in Pentecostalism or in the counter-culture.

The motif of glory should of course be safeguarded against whatever version of intoxication. To take just one of the influential images of revolt which haunt the imagination of our period, that of Dionysus: here the motifs of spontaneity and ecstasy are ambiguous. Beyond the more superficial intoxication of the god of the vine and of untrammeled vitality—à la Zorba the Greek—the initiate into the cult is drawn into the true mania where dance and immolation are inseparable. Some of our other contemporary scenarios for ecstasy and creativity are similarly seductive. But they all point to a craving for spontaneity occasioned by the character of our society, a thirst for liberation of the self, which the Christian sacrament of regeneration has every resource to satisfy. As a matter of fact the New Testament church elaborated the symbolics of its message and its ceremonies in just such a situation and in confrontation with just such powerful mythologies as those of Dionysus. Our liturgical practise today may well accommodate more persuasive images of the mystery of selfhood and its transformation responsive to our own categories of alienation.

One other contemporary mythology or dream of innocence may be cited. A French author with his eye on the student revolts in Paris in 1968 has studied the "oneiric scenarios" of the counter-culture as there disclosed. One recurrent motif—more political but no less ambiguous than that of Dionysus—was the old dream of the revolt of the beggars or the vagabonds.[2] The classic instance was that of the Peasants' Revolt in 1525. Fumes of eschatological hysteria seemed to rise out of the ground itself. Thomas Müntzer preached his mystique of the New Man. In an appeal to primitive Christianity, love and freedom from all law were reconcilable with violence. The movement ended in the sanguinary anarchy of Münster. But the basic model of the brotherhood of the forlorn and the alienated is a perennial one and has its contemporary appeal in our setting.

One could identify other underground mystiques and myths that cast their spell on the imagination of our time. Perhaps the most important is that of Apocalypse testified so widely in literature and the arts today. The vision of an End can mean catastrophe to some, a new heaven and earth to others; it represents an otherworldly escape for some and the fulfillment, the harvest of time for others; it is found as an obsessive delusion in mental hospitals and as a nourishing dream of saints and martyrs. In any case the contemporary rediscovery of the daemonic and the surreal dimensions of existence demands dramatic expression. So much so that, as a counter-impulse in religion and philosophy, we see a flight from time and history. Evidently dreams have power. Here again, a Christian apocalyptic is called for that can resolve these confusions. Only a theopoetic can order and baptize

2. Claude Mettra, *Le grand printemps des gueux* (Paris: A. Balland, 1969). See further, chap. 3 below.

these impulses that are shaping the future. We can be sure that as in the past the Spirit will prompt new tongues, new names, new songs to clarify these quests.

IV

The special quality of the experience of blessedness or glory in the Christian faith is related to the way in which evil is dealt with. There are various kinds and degrees of mystical joy or peace. The quality of such states is not just a matter of intensity. They can be intense but thin or morbid. They can be momentary or lasting. They can be isolated transports or they can be pervasive of the initiate's wider experience and relationships. They can represent the resolution of private psychic tension or of interpersonal and communal disorder.

The category of blessedness as the Christian understands it should not be confused with familiar forms of mystical transcendence. No doubt in their higher forms they reflect various levels of self-discipline and purgation. In this sense evil is assimilated and overcome. But Christian faith presumes to wrestle with the root evil of the race and the world, not only private but public. The costly victory here, assured though incomplete, fulfills all other glimpses of beatitude just because a deeper disorder is resolved.

As is suggested by the term *Kreuzseligkeit* Christian celebration is deepened by suffering and the early church's *hilarotes* (hilarity) is possible without irresponsibility. The term *Kreuzseligkeit* or "blessedness in the cross" does not connote a masochistic cult of suffering, though certain traditions of piety have sometimes been thus distorted. The experience recognizes the believer's participation in that divine operation in which ultimate evil is encountered and transmuted.

We speak about a theopoetic because the theme of divinity requires a dynamic and dramatic speech. Divinity has to do with the glory of God and the creature's participation in it. But this means participation in his life and activity and this is something other than passive mystical illumination or epiphanies of the sacred. The greatest transcriptions we have of human blessedness like that of Dante's golden rose are all social: they have to do with the panegyric of uncounted multitudes and universal harmony. The communion of saints represents the seraphic joy of the church triumphant in celebration of the travail and triumph of the church militant. The quality of such mystical initiation, anticipated in common experience, is far richer than that of our fragmentary aesthetic or esoteric moments of transcendence. Here too, transliminal experience, rather than being exceptional or even escapist, is interwoven with the daily fabric of existence so that glory is associated with both its labor and its redemptive costs.

This temper and the vision that supports it can meet the needs of those eventually disillusioned with other contemporary versions of transcendence or ecstasy. Such options are pursued today not only because our modern secular world would recover a sense of the sacred but also because it lacks the spiritual courage to affirm a more total vision. The so-called polytheism of our culture is a symptom both of new religious sensibility and of a limitation of faith.

Perhaps the greatest single contribution that a new theopoetic could make—whether for the liberal churches or for the Evangelicals, both alike limited by dated stereotypes, or for the many kinds of secular mystics—would be to repossess the mystery of the cross and its glory in a way that would speak to all.

2

The Recovery of the Sacred

There is a gestation proceeding in our epoch whose proper vehicles are symbolic and imaginative. Wide orders of response have long been inhibited or neglected, and men and women in a variety of situations are rediscovering aspects of the spontaneous, the sacred, and the mysterious.

The importance of this new climate should be recognized. The cultural consequences can be momentous. Even though many features of the many-sided impulse raise questions, we should give attention to the wider phenomenon. Though it may manifest itself in ways we have long associated with obscurantism and irrationality, with the occult and the orgiastic, even these may well call for a second look. At least they may throw a negative light on long-held assumptions about the normal and the reasonable.

Similarly we should be attentive to those new or renewed investigations of mystical, psychic, oneiric, or "primitive" phenomena which help us to orient ourselves in all these dimensions of the self and its powers. Though Western society and the church have had long experience of the disorders of the imagination and of destructive phantasies both individual and social, yet older canons and tabus may be unsuited to a new occasion.

The biblical legacy has of old transformed itself without loss through engagement with new cultural situations.

As the theater has widened, its resources have been evoked. Similarly the humanistic tradition of the West, indeed its rational and scientific tradition, should be hospitable to new impulses that may at first appear alien or even obscurantist. Even science and academic orthodoxy can be inhibited by older milestones of their advance.

The lack of comprehension of our situation cannot be better illustrated than by the admirable scientist Joseph Bronowski. In the concluding chapter of *The Ascent of Man* he writes: "I am infinitely saddened to find myself surrounded in the west by a sense of terrible loss of nerve, a retreat from knowledge into—into what? Into Zen Buddhism; into falsely profound questions about, Are we not really just animals at bottom; into extra-sensory perception and mystery. They do not lie along the line of what we are now able to know if we devote ourselves to it: an understanding of man himself."[1] He has remarked earlier, ". . . no beliefs can be built up in this century that are not based on science as the recognition of the uniqueness of man, and a pride in his gifts and works."[2]

It is far from my intention to disparage Bronowski's magnificent book, television series, and witness. He sets forth an unanswerable claim for science, intellect, human responsibility, and the open mind. But if he were present one would like to be playful with him. Be it noted that he can be as scornful of older religious legacies as he is of some contemporary mysticisms, characterizing the former as living "out of a ragbag of morals that come

1. Jacob Bronowski, *The Ascent of Man* (Boston and Toronto: Little, Brown & Co., 1973), p. 437.
2. Ibid., p. 432.

from past beliefs."[3] One would like to ask him if he has not preempted all human explorations and faculties for his own line of achievement. He manages to include great artists, visionaries, and prophets among his pioneers. Rather than being embarrassed as an apostle of science and empiricism by such figures as Shakespeare and Jesus he appropriates them for his roll call of rational liberators. No doubt Jesus was a liberator, but there are other kinds of bondage than ignorance, intellectual inertia, and cultural dogma.

Bronowski might have asked himself whence the deeper incentives arise for scientific curiosities and pragmatic applications. The history of science has something to say about this. Basic cultural apperception, our religious vision of man and nature, determines the play of intellect, the direction of mind and effort. Bronowski might also have recognized that exploration of the psyche and what he might have hesitated to call metaphysical reality can involve the same honesty with experience as the rational operations to which he assigns the ascent of man. Why should he not have conceded that an appropriate extension of investigation today might be to wisdoms of the soul, ancient and modern, Eastern and Western?

Not only for theology today but for all assessment of cultural realities and norms, due recognition must be given to the new intuitive and mystical sensibility, to new somatic and affectional perceptions, to the new religiosity and inwardness, to the new mythical consciousness. Rather than seeing these impulses as a loss of nerve or a repudiation of our best Western humanism we may rather find them signaling a return to the proper plenitude and

3. Ibid., p. 436.

diversity of our human nature as common to many epochs and climes.

What is in view here is much more than what has been called the counter-culture or the Age of Aquarius. These have been only particular and local symptoms of a wider event in our society. A broad spectrum of observation is called for which includes not only dissident cults but the surfacing of a more general shift of consciousness, not only mutations in the arts but in life-styles, not only incipient revolution in the aesthetic and symbolic order but also in social and political disaffection. All such changes can be summarized as a shift in our sense of reality. Of course, they proceed against resistance and their emergence is marked by particular conflicts in particular areas and disciplines.

In this situation the new impulses and their initiates and interpreters should be duly valued. I refer, for examples, to the initiates in Oriental religions, to those concerned with regimens of meditation, to the mythologues, the Jungians, the Dionysians, and to all those who explore the dynamics of consciousness and our commerce with reality whether by cultic ritual or by scientific measurement. All these at the very least widen our acquaintance with the mysteries of the self and help to free us from parochial assumptions and traditional mental habits and tabus.

What concerns me, however, is that all such explorations should be carried out in dialogue with the insights and accumulated wisdom of our own older religious traditions. The understandable iconoclasm which dominates so many of the new curiosities and disciplines should not lead to neglect of this body of experience and reflection. The fact that the Christian tradition has become identified with restrictive and oppressive cultural attitudes does not mean that it has no resources to offer in the new situation. Indeed the turn to more exotic sources of illumination in our time may be prompted not by what is insufficient or corrupted in Christianity but rather by a shrinking from what it still validly represents.

There are good reasons why much of the biblical tradition has seemed unavailable or indigestible for the contemporary interest in mysticism and depth-experience. It is understandable that these new explorations should have proceeded so long without benefit of clergy in this sense. But the time is now overdue in which the dialogue should be renewed.

Why is it that when available texts for meditative discipline today are gathered, early Christianity is represented chiefly by extracts from its heretical books? The fact is that contemporary mystics do not find what they want in either the New or the Old Testament. They may find isolated phrases from the Gospel of John but they are more at home with the apocryphal gospel of Thomas. The age-old universal appeal of pantheism or of some kind of secret wisdom appears today in new forms and biblically oriented piety and prayer seem insipid or confining. How can one explain that the Book of Psalms is passed over by those intent on a new spirituality?

It is not my purpose here to disparage the new impulse to inwardness and its thirst for reality. It is rather a question of keeping open the full scope of such quests. One can find other examples of the neglect or misunderstanding of the biblical tradition and of the resources it could contribute in this new climate. The interest today in comparative mythology, for example, tends to look elsewhere than to the Bible for its archetypes. Even when the myth and ritual of early Christianity are included, since the time of Sir James Frazer's *Golden Bough* they have been mistakenly merged with those of the ancient world and with the mystery cults of Roman paganism. The impulse to universalize the myths and archetypes of the race, together with their wisdom and illumination, has thus favored one particular focus and obscured the legacy of Israel.

It is relevant here to recall the similar issue that has recently arisen over the impressive labors of Claude Lévi-Strauss on the myths of preliterate societies in Latin America and North America. Paul Ricoeur has challenged his claim to universalize his conclusions. If Lévi-Strauss had investigated similarly the myths of such open societies as that of Israel his results would have been different.[4]

The general problem is highlighted by a recent review of Joseph Campbell's Bollingen volume, *The Mythic Image.*[5] The review is highly appreciative and I myself would be among the first to pay tribute to Campbell for his contributions as a mythographer and for his valuable participation in such discussions as those of the Society for the Arts, Religion and Contemporary Culture.[6] One feature of the comment in question points up the indigestible aspect of the biblical writings in general studies of mythology, and, I may add, in contemporary movements directed to mysticism and depth-experience. The re-

4. Claude Lévi-Strauss, "Structure et hermeneutique," *Le conflit des interpretations* (Paris, 1969), pp. 31–63, esp. pp. 44–53.

5. Joseph Campbell, *The Mythic Image* (Princeton: Princeton University Press, 1974).

6. Note also his editorship of its volume, *Myths, Dreams and Religion,* by Alan Watts, Norman Brown, Ira Progoff, Rollo May, Owen Barfield and others, which includes two chapters dealing with biblical material.

viewer, Iris V. Cully, concludes her remarks as follows:

> Upon reflection after closing the book, one becomes aware of some emphases more than others. To bring the biblical tradition into consonance with the whole, the Judaic illustrations come largely from heretical sources. . . . The scriptural (i.e. written) tradition is largely omitted. Christian quotations are made from the gnostic gospel of Thomas, with only a few from canonical materials . . . Christianity is represented largely through a mystical approach (Blake, medieval art). The Islamic tradition is sparsely represented. While this illustrates a Jungian approach to the understanding of the self in terms of archetypal dreams and myth, it neglects one total side of the human being, represented by the moral implications of the Covenant, the reconciling motiv in the death of Jesus, or the eight-fold path affirmed by the Buddha as the way toward enlightenment. This suggests little of the ethical significance in mythic images.
>
> This is not to say that such material should have been included in the book, but only to point out that even in so broad a survey of the religious impulse, one whole dimension can be lacking.[7]

But the problem with much contemporary mysticism and spirituality is that the adepts are not even aware that one whole dimension may be lacking. It would be too simple besides invidious to say that it is the ethical dimension that is lacking. Certainly such explorers or iconoclasts as Alan Watts, Gerald Heard, and Norman O. Brown have had ethical concerns. Indeed much of their motivation may in the first place arise out of revolt against the ethical deficiencies of the established faiths. No. The dimension too often missing is rather that of rootedness, creaturehood, embodied humanness.

7. Iris V. Cully, *The Review of Books and Religion* 4, no. 9 (Mid-June 1975): p. 11. Used by permission.

It is often urged that the biblical myth and "way" are different because man's relation to the gods is here seen in terms of history not psychology, the public theater and not the life of the soul, action not inwardness. This is only partly true. All religion has been related to the historical experience of tribe, cult, or visionary. On the other hand the covenant religion of Israel had its own dimension of private spirituality. Deeper than the criterion of "history" in the biblical orientation is the kind of humanness, the more total mystery of the self. The potentialities of the heart and soul of man, his active many-sided dealings with an inexhaustible creation, are opened up in the biblical charters. It is a question of reality and of how reality is located, and of how a full human reality is not truncated or forfeited.

It is in keeping with this understanding of reality that biblical religion from the beginning has been oriented to history, society, politics, with the consequent emphasis on obligation, law, and judgment. Even the otherwordliness that developed in some forms of Christianity could never entirely shed the social perspective. These pragmatic aspects of the faith are today widely held against it, the more so because Christianity has inevitably been involved for so long in the authoritative structures of the West.

For understandable reasons modern versions of enlightenment wish to transcend history if not to escape from it. But by so doing they forfeit some of their essential humanity. As with early gnosticism they weaken their roots in nature and in being itself. Even where contemporary sensibility celebrates a new naiveté with respect to the body, to natural forms, and to the cosmos itself, these epiphanies lack the robustness suggested in Genesis or the Book of Job.

I have said enough however to indicate the value I

assign to the new quests and illuminations of our time. What is needed today is more correlation of all such findings with our older traditions. My rubric of "theology and theopoetic" suggests the task. Since the tradition is so widely under attack in the current situation it is proper that current proposals be sifted and scrutinized.

I return to my observation that men and women today in a variety of situations are rediscovering aspects of the spontaneous, the sacred, and the mysterious. So insistent is the demand in many quarters that any momentary release with its particular version of transcendence takes on immense authority. If a person is starving he prizes the first food at hand. In this situation mysticism is like calf-love. The youth is in love with love. The uninitiated are dazzled by the Spirit.

The opportunity of our time is that depth is again calling to depth. The ambiguity of the occasion is that any unwanted release may carry the credentials of salvation. The available satisfies. The immediate takes on priority over all other illumination. Intensity is mistaken for quality: voltage without amperage.

Such momentary epiphanies and disclosures of reality are to be honored but it is their scope that is in question. Explosions of meaning, pinpoints of ecstatic vision, they slake a psychic craving but provide no orientation. Indeed it is part of their prestige that they seem to focus all truth; their very intensity precludes further exploration.

In this situation the Christian should be even more attentive than others to the gestation in question. He knows that individuals and societies live from deep springs of faith and dream. He knows that the more visible orders of the world are continually nourished, shaped, and transformed by hidden powers. He knows that the fateful operations of these powers are brought to light in prophetic augury and parable.

Thus the believer should be alert to all visions and oracles of the time, not least to those which rebuke his own impoverishment. But the time comes when dream must be measured by dream and revelation by revelation, and all tested by a total human experience. He can be sure that authentic new empowerments will be validated by such tests, but the Christian will ask questions about their scope and ultimacy. The Spirit is not to be quenched, yet the spirits should be tested.

Just because consciousness is expanded is no guarantee of genuine human liberation. Even alleged cosmic consciousness can be basically superficial when measured by human extremity. Horizons opened by Oriental disciplines or planetary vision, however welcome and instructive, can still be parochial. Initiation into archetypal mysteries, subliminal labyrinths, or the kaleidoscopic phantasmata induced by *soma* or the mushroom may similarly by-pass the radical human problem, which has to do with our waking life in the sunlight and our choices and relations.

Though contemporary rediscovery of the sacred claims no total world-understanding one can appreciate this reticence. It is to be welcomed at least that the category of the transcendent should be recovered in our time. Though God is not invoked it is no small matter that a secular age can speak of the "naming of the gods." The diverse hierophanies testified to by the contemporary imagination suggest the much discussed new "polytheism." The thick crust of worldliness and its obsessive practicalities is broken through by impulses of wonder and playfulness. This appears to augur a new age of faith. At least this is a big step beyond the "death of God" even if it falls short of a more total vision.

It is true that the widely manifested turn beyond the rational to phantasy can take distempered forms. The initiate and the cult are vulnerable to the exotic, the occult, and the sensational. And they are specially vulnerable to the iconoclastic for its own sake. There are no symbols and scenarios of the oneiric universe which are so intoxicating as those of refusal and revolt and even of ravage and destruction.

Fortunately this daimonic and dynamic impulse can surface in more healthful ways. It can relate itself constructively to the ordering visions of the past and their arts and rituals. But such synthesis is blocked so long as those great legacies remain obscured or are even seen as the enemy.

A vital theopoetic can renew the biblical faith for a living encounter with the deeper currents of the age. But at the same time our age must purge itself of its own complacencies. Every modern impulse of emancipation from the Renaissance down to the liberation movements of today has been ambiguously motivated. The causes of humanism and liberty have thrown off successive yokes all too often without allowing themselves to be judged. So the visionaries and iconoclasts of our time may need to be reminded of a higher instance.

If indeed we are on the threshold of a new age of faith and if new myth-making powers manifest themselves it remains to be seen whether they truly answer to our human condition generally and not just the vagaries of our moment. One test of this will be their openness to all dimensions of human need and all inherited wisdoms.

The cults and ecstacies and liberations of today aspire

toward a recovery of innocence. Often this represents a convulsive effort to throw off the psychological and moral miasmas of a sick society. In place of the Law, the Intellect, the Censor, and the Shadow (associated with Jehovah, Nay-Saying, and Death) the stifled impulse of the heart wrestles for a restored naiveté and spontaneity.

On the one hand this means a fresh sensibility vis-à-vis nature, labor, instinct, and play. For one example here I need only mention the poetry of Gary Snyder. On the other hand it means a revolt against long inbred cultural controls and their myths, political, sexual, ethnic, economic. But these illuminations and emancipations can only be fragmentary and gratuitous unless they recognize and come to grips with a more obstinate kind of bondage. Though the Bible sets the terms of a deeper innocence and its cost, its more total vision should not be disallowed.

3

Contemporary Mythologies and Theological Renewal

I can link up with what has so far been said by a brief summary. In any given situation theology should relate itself not only to the philosophical ideas of the time but to its symbolic life and creative impulses. While theology properly takes the form of clear thinking about God, the faith, and the world, it has a basic substratum of imaginative grasp on reality and experience. The great theologians have always had this plastic and dynamic element in their thought, and it has been continuous with and nourished by the social imagination of their epoch. The thought of Aquinas was indebted to the visionary structures that inspired Dante, as that of Augustine was to those that inspired Neo-Platonism. There is a correspondence between Milton's *De Doctrina Christiana* and his *Paradise Lost*. In our time when the theological tradition has lost so much of its cogency it is particularly important that it should redefine itself in relation to the dominant myths, dreams, images of the age, that is, with the contemporary quest-patterns of a changing world.

I

This is not just a question of the strategies of communication. Nor does it mean that the Gospel is to be conformed to the world and its ideologies. It is a question of being able to identify with the sensibility of today, even though the believer knows his own ground and remains loyal to it. The Christian ought to be able to say to the multitudes of our time: "I know how you feel; I know how you register things. I also can resonate to your revolts, cravings, visions, neuroses. I have been there myself." But to do this the Christian and the theologian should accept initiation into the deeper vicissitudes of our years, the changing spiritual climate, with the consequent changes in all that has to do with communication, language, arts, and rituals. In this process theology itself will have to go through a transmutation. Its proper authority can only be made good if it comes to terms with the ruling metaphors and idioms of its setting. This requires visionary capacity at least as potent as that of the prevailing secular dreams and idolatries.

I can illustrate this as a student of the New Testament and the early transmutations of the Gospel. When Paul and other missionaries to the Gentiles went out into the cities of Asia Minor and Greece they had to appeal to a different kind of culture. The impact and meaning of their message depended on a changed rhetoric and appropriate symbol. The terms and categories of their witness had to be modulated to awaken response in a different theater with its own acoustics and its own imaginative repertoire. Their words and their ceremonies carried over into the hearts of men because they could do this.

The apostles did not forfeit their faith in this transition nor the faith of those who first proclaimed the Gospel in Palestine. But the message was transmuted in a new climate. The point is that they could do this because they were at home in the dreams and hungers, psychological and political, the mysteries and mythologies, of the Hellenistic world. The letters of Paul took hold of the readers at this deep level, through all the potent layers of the self, especially the unconscious and the prerational. So it has been with the more creative witnesses always. They have known not only how to clarify ideas but to give signals that could awake a deep resonance in the hearts of men.

It is in this order of imagination and social dream, moreover, that we find the bridge between the theologian and action in his time, between theology and politics. When the Word is linked with the dynamic mythology of an age the faith is secured against privatism. On the other hand, when faith is not thus exposed it becomes devitalized. A traditional theology, oriented to older vicissitudes of the church militant, encourages an evangelical pietism or an ineffective liberalism. A theopoetic oriented to today's struggle with the principalities and powers can overcome their bondage, exorcize their evil, and shape the human future.

There is a wide misunderstanding about what constitutes effective Christian social action. For the militants the New Testament—apart from Jesus' driving out the money changers—is almost a total loss. On their view such action can only be carried out in the streets or at the barricades in direct confrontation with some particular power structure. This view infects a great deal of liberation theology. Such activism is vulnerable to sub-Christian motivations, and in fact is often carried out in association with allies who have only their own partisan interests to serve. Such direct action may nevertheless serve a necessary pragmatic end in a limited context, but it should be recognized that it is a power strategy, a conflict of wills, and does not change men's minds.

An effective social action will operate at a deeper level where the wrestling is with the loyalties, banners, and spells that rule a way of life and its institutions. In such an engagement no doubt occasions of public confrontation will arise. When they do Christian action will have a symbolic or dramatic character, enforcing its deeper persuasions. Early Christianity was more like guerilla theater than social revolution, but it overthrew principalities and powers. When Jesus drove out the money changers they were no doubt back again the next day or the next week. But the episode was an acted parable and evoked the powerful theocratic vision of the prophets.

At the other end of the scale is the otherworldly tradition which, appealing to the New Testament, would trust to evangelism and piety to order and regenerate the common life.

It is true that if we look at the New Testament history in an anachronistic way we seem to see a movement devoted to soul-saving, indifferent to politics, slavery, and other social patterns. But actually it was a guerilla operation which undermined social authority by profound persuasions. What no overt force could do it did by spiritual subversion at the level of the social imagination of the polis and the provinces of the empire. It was a case of liturgy against liturgy, of myth against myth. And these liturgies and myths had their institutional embodiments. Consider the uproar in Ephesus when the Gospel had deflated the market for the sacred images of its great goddess, Artemis, and the burning of the magic books to the value of fifty thousand pieces of silver.

So also in Jesus' own ministry the summons was related to the dynamic mythology of his people and thus had implicit political or theocratic bearings. It is a travesty to interpret salvation as represented in the Gospels as a matter of otherwordly soul-saving. Those who followed him knew themselves sharers in God's final purification and blessing of his people, and so of the world. The ethical and social implications and goals of the movement are unmistakable though obscured for us by its apocalyptic vision of the world process.

Our argument has begun with the plea that Christian witness must engage our times at the level of its unconscious axioms and inherited symbolics and not only at that of its ideas. Since such cultural imagery is deep-rooted and powerful it can only be effectively encountered if Christianity draws on its own arsenal of vision. But this eloquence will not be persuasive unless it is lived out and unless its archetypes are quickened and reshaped in the encounter. Such encounter takes place both in depth and at the public level.

The war of myths or contest with the idols which goes on in the hidden dramas of the heart can also come to open conflict in the life of institutions and society. But when such public clashes emerge it is important that the action and suffering of the church militant bear witness to and reinforce the deeper persuasions of the Spirit.

A revitalized message comes out of drastic involvement in the life-options of the situation. This need not be only the involvement of the picket line or the barricade. There are many areas of solidarity with human scandal and many forms of private and costly wrestling with pervasive tyrannies old and new. Such dramatic encounters in the public theater as we have seen in the cases of Dietrich Bonhoeffer and Martin Luther King both clarify and are nourished by countless more obscure loyalties. But imaginative solidarity with our modern disorders informs all such resistance both public and private. It is in this crucible that the powerful new rhetoric and witness are forged, and the revolution of images.

It is related to this that the civil rights marches and demonstrations were reinforced by hymns and spiritual songs old and new as in the vigils of the early church. Bonhoeffer's harried congregations were sustained by newly eloquent apocalyptic imagery in hymn, sermons, liturgy, and letter. So in the early church there was much of what we would call subversive songs, guerilla theater, underground messages, and political graffiti. The empire did not know what to do with this clandestine movement whose dreams were more universal and contagious than those of the Sibyls and the oracles or of Vergil himself.

II

What is the character of the new outlook and sensibility with which a contemporary theopoetic must come to terms? We are often instructed as to the intellectual and scientific revolution in our period. We also know about social and economic changes. But here we are interested in more elusive features of the situation: the reality-sense, the governing apperceptions, the sensorium. If I speak again of the myths and dreams of the culture I am only appealing to what anthropologists concern themselves with in the societies which they study.

But first we do well to note the various evidences of a dissolution of older patterns. I enumerate briefly some of the symptoms and indices as they exhibit themselves for various observers.

Certain over-all trends in the arts point not only to changing optics but to deeper shifts in consciousness. We have to ask what these radical mutations and impulses are saying to us about the spirit of the times. It is clear that there is some relocation going on for many in all that has to do with meaning and the sense of reality. I have in mind especially the more iconoclastic arts: the theater of the absurd and its sequels, the *nouveau roman,* and those fictions which reflect changed perspectives on space and time, the new dimensions opened up in contemporary cinema. Modern experience seems to be driving the painter beyond surrealism to abstract impressionism, the poet to "projective verse," and the public arts to phantasy and the psychedelic.

Next we note the youth culture with its special celebrations and symbols. In discussing the counter-culture Theodore Roszak has stressed youth's rejection of the "myth of objective consciousness." This meant a return to spontaneity, imagination, the wisdom of the body, cosmic rhythms, and uninhibited immediacy of awareness. Though we may recognize today that the Age of Aquarius is in some ways already dated, yet the larger transformation of consciousness which it represented is still very much with us.

One further aspect of this has been the revolt against the academy. More widely than in the counter-culture we have seen an erosion of authority of the "objective consciousness" of learning, of critical analysis, of departmental specialization. The student chafes at academic demands not only because he may identify them with passports to an Establishment which he suspects, but because the ethos and savor of the rational tradition seem insipid to him.

At a more sophisticated if not more fundamental level we note in the field of philosophy the revolt against metaphysics, against "objective thinking"—with Heidegger a return beyond Plato and Aristotle to the pre-Socratics, to the authentic wisdom of Being; or with existentialism generally, a focus on reality in terms of the freedom and intentionality of a deeper self.

Finally we may note the observations of social psychologists as well as critics of art and literature bearing on this question of the modern self and its sense of identity. We hear of "Protean" man and his loss of center or the attenuation of his sense of personal reality. Bourgeois man is troubled not only by the erosion of his traditional external structure of order and authority, but by an inner emptiness. To return to the modern theater and novel, we find a recurrent fascination with masquerades of identity, the dramas of the psyche, the stripping away of mask behind mask. All such alienation may take on aspects of dread and nihilism, but it can also be looked on as a radical process of emancipation. Thus we can understand the ambiguity of the most iconoclastic arts of today, and we can better perceive the motives of much convulsive social and political behavior.

Under these five heads I have summarized certain symptoms and indices of a radical change of sensibility in our time. No doubt there are many who will not have had experience of them and who will minimize their importance. By the same token those unalerted to the deeper transformations going on will be unable to put particular behaviors or idioms in their right context. To such circles the query of Bob Dylan is apt: "But you don't know what's happening here, do you Mr. Jones?" But theology and faith should be able to interpret the wider mutation, and should come to terms with this new order of experience and with its implicit myths and hungers.

Another way to come at the situation is to note certain typical representations of it.

1) "A new Middle Age." A generation ago Berdyaef wrote a book with this title. The English edition carried the title, *The End of Our Age.* His theme was that the West was moving out of the age of rationality and the Enlightenment into an age of imaginative depth, of mythological mentality like that of the Middle Ages. He saw

this as a deepening of consciousness and not as a loss or a retrogression. Already in his time a movement among English and Welsh poets called "Apocalypse" corresponded to motifs in German expressionism and a wider surrealism. This whole change in our Western register of experience has moved a great deal further today.

2) Another formulation is that of Marshall McLuhan. Our situation is characterized as one of "weightlessness." All older categories are confounded. This accounts for a widespread feature of our arts: that of gratuity, the celebration of the momentary, the happening, the isolated epiphany, the improvisation, the *acte gratuite*. So we get the turn to phantasy and its unrehearsed novelties, its balloons and colors, or the return to *homo ludens* and to play as the true reality.

3) Still another characterization is in terms of nakedness. For good or ill our modern man is stripped of his inherited protections and shelters, whether of customs, ideas, or myths. So we get titles like that of Erich Heller, *The Disinherited Mind*, or of von Holthusen, *Der unbehauste Mensch.* But this can be looked on as an advantage. Our naked humanity, stripped of all the buffers and insulations of culture, is thus all the more immediately exposed to Being itself, to the primal mystery. What we call personality gives way to a more authentic identity or greater self capable of spontaneity and ecstasy. Thus Rilke has been called the "poet of our time" for in his work he explicitly transcribes this ultimate envelopment in the Real and the consequent transmutation of the world and the Word.

4) Again, the new phase is defined in terms of the metaphor of depth. The fate of the West has led us to an exploration of inwardness, of subjectivity. The mod-

ern arts show the obsession with psychologism, the maladies and the mysteries of the psyche, the uncovering of the prerational and the arcane and of the oneiric or dream-life within. In the Renaissance the exploration was that of the outward, the rational, the objective. Today the direction is reversed, and this can mean that old myths and archetypes of the spirit, Eastern and Western, again become available.

III

The indices I have cited and the various formulations of the situation all help us to define the new sensibility, to know better where we are today, and to realize what is going on. So far as theology is concerned three things stand out.

For one thing appeal to the past becomes a problem when there is so much emphasis on iconoclasm and improvisation. "I must invent myself," is a recurrent motif. This dethroning of old authorities and worlds of meaning is well brought out in Robert Creeley's poem, "The Dishonest Mailman":

> They are taking all my letters, and they
> put them into a fire.
>
>   I see the flames, etc.
> But do not care, etc.
>
> They burn everything I have, or what little
> I have. I don't care, etc.
>
> The poem supreme, addressed to
> emptiness—this is the courage
>
> necessary. This is something
> quite different.[1]

1. Robert Creeley, *For Love: Poems, 1950–1960* (New York: Scribner, 1962), p. 29. Reprinted by permission.

The letters do not go through, either those that he sends or those that he should receive. Communication is sabotaged. He is in the position of Kafka's "K" whose appeals are frustrated and whose messages are blocked. He is thrown back on creative improvisation. He must invent himself in a vacuum. He must break through into another reality. "Je est un autre." ("This is something quite different"). We are familiar with "emptiness" as a revelatory category in Zen.

We should not press the meaning of the poem too far. However it is a good example of "projective verse" (and of some wider circles in the arts and in mysticism) which looks for salvation in an ultimate creativity. The pure voice sought must be uncontaminated by old echoes, ideas, or images. Old fables or myths, including religious faiths, are seen as imprisoning except as they may be drawn on as cyphers for the pure extramundane dream of creativity with its two aspects of iconoclasm and transcendence.

We need not look so far to find evidences today that inherited structures of the past are a problem. If theology is to renew itself in the face of this attitude to tradition then the Christian givens of the past must be brought forward in a new register, in a new contemporary vision, so that they can speak to this ambiguous emptiness. But this is what the "new hermeneutic" is all about, not least in its wrestling with the premetaphysical categories of Heidegger.

In the second place this new sensibility requires that the Christian faith be brought to speech again in the modes, genres, and styles of contemporary spirituality. Testimonies of the Spirit in our theater will have their own secular character and idiom. Theology as in the time of the New Testament will take form on the basis of prophecies, exclamations, aphorisms, words out of the ordeal, letters from prison, watch-words of the Resistance, beatitudes and woes and parables in the worldly idiom of our own setting and our own involvement.

In the third place a renewed theological language will relate itself, or better, will find itself related to those contemporary symbols and myths which are gestating in the secular world today. Just as the earliest Christians found a wider utterance for their message by repossession of Gnostic idiom and divine models like those of Hercules and Dionysus, so today new vehicles will be found in such quests as those for the hidden self or an ecological mystique. To quote Myron Bloy here speaking with reference to the counter-culture:

> It is clear, that if the church cannot help the counter-culture to celebrate existence in the symbols of its tradition—in symbols which are . . . commensurate with the mystery and complexity of existence even though their power is now problematic—then we may be committing the young by default to a symbolic resolution of their quest which is not only less satisfying but also, as history has shown, culturally demonic.[2]

The Society for the Arts, Religion and Contemporary Culture in recent years focused its discussions successively upon the cultural themes of the clown, the daimonic, and the grotesque. The figure of the clown in literature, painting, and film has had extraordinary resonance in our period, evoking both the orders of the sacred and the redemptive. The category of the daimonic, highlighted earlier by Paul Tillich and more recently by Rollo

2. Myron Bloy, "Culture and Counter-Culture" in *Commonweal,* 17 January 1969, p. 496.

May, is highly illuminating with respect to both the creative and the disturbing in the mystiques of our contemporaries. The order of the grotesque in the graphic arts and in literature evidences the morbid and the diabolical that are parasitic on the life of the imagination and therefore of cultural forms. The good artist today portrays it to exorcize it, and is thus in the line of the devil dances of tribal communities. In all of these areas we have dramatizations of the modern experience which invite a theological reading and which offer themselves to a contemporary Christian symbolic.

IV

As a sequel to the student demonstrations in Paris, in 1968 a publishing house initiated a series of books under the label of "R" standing for *Revolte.* These authors studied perennial fables and models of spiritual iconoclasm and adventure as a way of clarifying the present. The first deals with the mythology of the vagabond, the tramp, and the gypsy. As I have noted in my first chapter, it examines the Peasants' Revolt of 1525 under the title, *Le grand printemps des gueux* ("The great springtime of the beggars").[3] Here we had a time when, as a reviewer in *Le Monde* observes, there was a great cleavage in society and religion. Here as today was a mystique nourished by hungers, cries, and violence, but also animated with a revolutionary fervor and love like a mania. Its prophets were moved by a dream of a new humanity linked with a return to primitive Christianity. But this dream is also one of today and tomorrow. Remembering as we do the blood bath in which it ended we see how

3. Claude Mettra, *Le grand printemps des gueux* (Paris: A. Balland, 1969).

important it is that this recurrent scenario should be directed to a better fullfillment in our time.

The second book in the series inquires into the perennial fascination of the freebooter, the beachcomber, and the pirate.[4] Here too is a mythology of refusal and of aspiration for the absolute. As the reviewer notes:

> The life of the freebooter bids farewell to the city and to society, and flies toward the dawn of the first and last day of the world. . . . Any city is a dagger in his heart.

Here we have the seductive dream of an absolute liberty, and it takes the sea as its proper theater.

> The ocean becomes a daedalus where the lost ships seek their own way as one seeks to decipher an enigma. . . . The pirate lives in a sacred world where sacrilege, cruelty, pillage, assassination are acted out like incantatory rites. He is fascinated by the beauty of the devil. The sea is an allegory of eternity aspired after by the sea-robber.[5]

The reviewer notes that this imagery echoes that of French writers like Rimbaud, Lautréamont, and Perse. But he also observes that the images which cast their spell on all such seekers speak to all of us because they suggest the forbidden, the arcane, and the unappeased.

We recognize the power of all such mythologies of innocence and liberation in our time, and their obscure relation to genuine versions of salvation. Theology should be able to reorder all such antinomian impulses and empathize with their "oneiric scenarios," appreciating as we

4. Gilles Lapouge, *Les pirates* (Paris: A. Balland, 1969).
5. Francois Bott, *Le Monde*, Selection Hebdomadaire, no. 1109, January 22–28, 1970, p. 11.

do how the codes and prison shutters of the modern city become stifling.

These last examples suggest the more disturbing aspects of the imaginative climate of yesterday but also of today. As in the early sixteenth century so in our own disordered time multitudes can be swept away by sorceries that rise like fumes out of the deepest underground of our society. It is as though a whole migration could be lured right out of history by pied pipers with their visions of innocence and the garden of Eden.

All creative crises carry these kinds of ambiguities and dangers. The important thing is that the Christian faith should be reshaped in the same crucible where our secular voices arise. The religious tradition should be involved in the struggle and the risks. So it will find its own authentic voice. It may then give wings to the groping aspirations which otherwise take destructive forms.

The modern world has had a problem with authority—with the father-figure, Nobodaddy, the censor, the law, controls, and morals. If particular inherited intimidations are evidently spurious, why not all? Their nebulous sanctions betray their illegitimacy, whether priests or judges, whether Jupiter or Jehovah.

So pervasive and transcendent is this matter of authority that it could not but take on mythical attributes. Now for long these have been widely cast as evil. Whole scenarios portray the tyrannies, the deceptions, and the final overthrow of the enslaving powers. It is true that oppression can be directly combatted. But where the tyrant has such an appanage of mythical cohorts and demons he can only be effectively opposed by a corresponding mythology, a mythology of autonomy and innocence. The will is even more fertile in fabulations and dramatizations than the passions. Every victim, indeed every criminal (cf. the writings of Jean Genêt) justifies himself not only rationally but viscerally and histrionically.

But what if the modern world's problem with authority is infected with a willing self-deception? What if controls and limits are in the nature of things and to be acknowledged? More specifically, what if the father figure, Jehovah, does not permit himself to be travestied and if conscience, guilt, and forfeit are not to be psychologized away? Then our scenarios of emancipation and innocence only compound the evasion.

The Old Testament Jehovah and so the God of Christendom is the chief pretext and hidden issue in all this. Our humanistic tradition thinks to have an easy case in arraigning his favoritism and his bloodthirsty dealings in the Old Testament and his wrath and jealousy and penalties in the New. From its untroubled standpoint, however, no account is taken of the radical jeopardies of the human lot. Nor is justice done to the parables, hyperboles, and dramatizations of the biblical portrayals. The volcanic forces of human nature and history require austere and shocking transcription. It is all very well for a favored culture to humanize the gods, or for an aesthetic or mystical elite to locate salvation in the powers of the self. But the biblical peoples must wrestle as of old with the anarchy that threatens the human order, public and private.

In this light authority is inexorable and man's ultimate security. So in the case of the individual, the yoke of obligation both defines the creature and assures his place in existence. Over against all plausible modern emancipations from the law and the censor it is well to be reminded by W. H. Auden that "none of us shall escape whipping."

4

Traditional Pieties and the Religious Imagination

In the foregoing I have argued the proper role of the imagination in theology and the religious life, and its special necessity in a period like ours when the religious traditions are confronted with powerful new impulses demanding symbolic and mythic expression. In this chapter I wish to inquire about the resistances offered at various levels to the aesthetic and dramatic dimensions of faith both in our culture and in our churches.

As I have suggested, the rightful place of the imagination in religion is subject to much confusion. It is set over against the reason and looked on as merely decorative. Or it is set over against the will and looked on as frivolous. It can even be set over against revelation itself and looked on as idolatrous. To defend the imagination in the life of faith one has almost to begin over again with some new name for it. Coleridge went a long way to rescue it as an essential dimension of all knowing and apprehension. But we still have romantic ideas about it as something separably aesthetic and irresponsible.

But this view blocks any real understanding of the Spirit and its workings. Certainly man's deepest apprehensions of the world and the gods, or of God himself, have always been poetic in the sense of symbolic and metaphorical. All the great ways of life of mankind and of particular tribes have been based on decisive hierophanies or disclosures of the sacred through which the transcendent related itself to creaturely circumstances and language.

If imagination plays such a necessary part in religion a touchstone for the vitality of theology will be its attitude to the symbolic order and to the creative impulses, images, and dreams of men. I wish therefore to turn to the topic of religion and the arts, for it is in this area that one can observe the resistances of which I have spoken to the deeper dynamics of faith. The ethos and mental habit of our religious tradition have been insensitive to the aesthetic dimension whether in the church or in the wider society.

The pragmatic character of our American society has widely conditioned and limited artistic expression in our religious institutions as elsewhere. This may be particularly true of our Protestant and especially our nonliturgical churches. Even Catholic liturgy and devotion have accommodated themselves to our ethos, more active than contemplative. Our Protestant population has indeed had its own forms of ceremonial expression and its own imaginative piety. But these have been so sober that they have often failed to satisfy the human need for celebration and for spontaneity. Thus in the past compensations can be recognized: on the one hand in the rites and emblems of fraternal orders, or on the other in recurrent explosions associated with revivals, or the founding of utopian communities. Even such a wide-ranging movement as that of transcendentalism can thus be understood. In our own day such revolts and reactions take on an even more diverse character.

But even such reactions against the basic patterns and controls, psychological and aesthetic, have lacked in dramatic or mythic power. The pieties of the fathers had been undernourished since the time of Jonathan Edwards, and natural spontaneity was inhibited. Creative artistic impulse in church and culture was subdued to practicalities. We hear more about ingenuity than imagination, and about inventors and tinkerers than about artists.

In some legacies of American Protestantism, reason shaped faith at the expense of more vital and plastic expression. In other quarters it was dogma. More pervasively it was the predominance of moralism over spirituality. Even the nobler forms of moralism or ethical culture can be uncongenial to the artistic sensibility. In what can be remembered as the great days of the student Christian movement in the colleges—the days of the conferences at Northfield and Silver Lake, and the period of the Student Volunteer Movement with its goal, "The Evangelization of the World in This Generation"—some will still recall the powerful voice of John R. Mott. He began his typical address to his great audiences with the words: "Christianity first and last is a matter of the Will!"

I

On this question of the attitude to the arts in our religious tradition I trust I may be allowed a personal retrospect. In the early fifties Marvin Halverson wished to set forth a platform or apologia for his Department of Worship and the Arts, established in 1951 in the National Council of Churches. At that time I was a member of his Committee on Literature along with Cleanth Brooks, W. H. Auden, Stanley R. Hopper, Nathan A. Scott, Jr., and others. Halverson wished to justify further financing of his department in order to advance his own creative initiative especially in making contact with secular artists and inviting their collaboration.

It was not enough that his office should serve as a kind of artistic conscience for the churches in all that had to do with their architecture, stained glass, hymnals, and religious drama. What was needed was a soundly theological underpinning for the churches' encounter with culture generally and with the best writers and artists of the time. His supporter, Paul Tillich, had recently called for a vanguard of Christian theologians, artists, and critics who would both reshape the aesthetic and the liturgy of the churches and represent a bridge to the best imaginative life of the period.

A statement of mine was discussed, supplemented, and then adopted. It was here pointed out that the arts, good and bad, old and new, the fine arts and the media, all for better or worse are peculiarly the carriers of meaning and value in society. The encounter of the Gospel with the world, whether in evangelism, education, preaching, or theology, requires a deep appreciation of and initiation into the varied symbolic expressions of the culture. It was urged that individuals and groups live by their images and dreams, and that it is harder to change the archetypes, symbols, and myths of men than it is to change their ideas and doctrines. On the positive side the church was reminded that "much of modern literature and art represent a momentous struggle in the modern soul to recover depth and wholeness, to reaffirm personal responsibility in the face of dehumanization, to find a true order behind our modern anarchy . . . and so to prepare the way for a renewed human community."[1]

In 1961 Halverson gave up his post with the National

1. "The Church, the Arts and Contemporary Culture," a five-page statement, "approved by the Executive Board of the Division of Christian Life and Work of the National Council of Churches on October 4, 1955," and commended to the churches for study.

Council of Churches and sought wider extraecclesiastical contacts and support for his goals by founding what is now the Society for the Arts, Religion and Contemporary Culture. Alfred Barr was its first president. Shortly thereafter the NCCC through its then President J. Irwin Miller—a layman deeply committed to the arts—appointed a special committee on the Council's Role in the Field of Religion and the Arts. This committee was headed by Joseph Sittler and included Roger Ortmayer, Robert Seaver, Robert Tangeman, myself, and others. We drew up a report which incorporated a large part of my earlier statement. This was submitted to the General Board of the NCCC, meeting in October, 1963. It is especially to one episode in this session that I wish to call attention.

The board, a body of at least a hundred delegates, without dissent approved the report which carried with it a proposal for a reorganized Department of the Arts. The work of this department was subsequently carried on in an imaginative way for a decade by Roger Ortmayer. But there was one moment in the discussion of this action which was both interesting and revealing. It had to do with the financing of the new program. One board member asked whether the funds assigned to it could not better be allocated to the Council's department of evangelism. Why, he implied, should the churches give this kind of attention to the arts?

At this point Sittler, Robert Baker, and I answered that if it was a question of evangelism in the twentieth century, no more crucial engagement could be found than at the point of the symbolic media and images of the age. As our report had stated:

> Here we have a concrete and ready opportunity to challenge and expose the unexamined errors of our producing

> and consuming contemporaries in all that concerns their values, loyalties, way of life and assumptions in connection with the novels they read, the plays and films they see, the music they play and hear, the buildings in which they live, work and worship, the social symbols they revere, the dreams and fables, indeed the myths, they feed upon. All this plays a large part in the inner life, the color of the self, of the modern individual, from the cultural model of the adult to the hero-paradigm of the child. Here we have the "chambers of imagery" (Ezekiel 8:12) in the heart. Needless to say, we have to deal here with the mass-media of the great public as well as with the traditional arts and diverse cultural legacies. Moreover, the confusions of the believer are as often open to correction as are the confusions of those outside the churches. What is involved here is no less than a Christian criticism of life, and no such task is possible without an appeal to theological insights.

It was also pointed out to the questioner and to the board that in any case the main funding of the new program in the arts was to be provided out of private sources and thus would not burden the Council's general budget. This was not an unimportant consideration in the board's favorable action. But it had been evident that some of the delegates of the churches questioned any such concern with the arts, even if they paid their own way. What has Zion to do with Bohemia?

II

Those who have sought to awaken an artistic conscience in the religious institutions have widely met this kind of incomprehension. I need not cite here the struggle in Catholicism at home and abroad against the factory-produced stereotypes and pious clutter that filled so many of its churches. In Protestantism a corresponding mail-order religious art still widely obtains. What is more serious is the mind-set which counts such matters unimportant. It is not recognized that vitality in faith is inseparable from vitality in its vehicles of expression, and that truth in worship is inseparable from care, excellence, and honesty in the media of worship. Beyond this is the ever pressing need to relate such media and their symbols to a changing world. Pioneers in these matters have not had an easy time.

To return to my restrospect: one could find the same kind of disparagement or misconception of the arts in those years at many levels. As a village pastor I met it in the objection to having even square-dancing in the parish hall. This was no doubt motivated by old-time respect for the house of God. But there was also an unfortunate carry-over of disesteem for the sensuous or the innovative. A study of the grass roots religious culture of our American life would be highly revealing. It would show many contradictions. In the village church in question, as in school, home, Grange, and lodge, a critic could find many evidences of a barren aesthetic. Yet what seem the banal arts of the folkways can be deceiving to the outsider. They often carry intense meaning to some at least where the older cultural patterns continue.

The question as to the aesthetics of Middle America and its vicissitudes could lead us far. The topic is inseparable from that of wider cultural and social forces. One is reminded here of the portrayal of civic demoralization and babbitry in John Updike's *Poorhouse Fair*. But any more factual reportage would have to take account of those inconsistencies and exceptions which human nature always exhibits. In the village I refer to, in any case, Main

Street could show many redeeming features: survivals of high taste in some of the older families, musical instruction and choral training by a French artist trained in the Paris Conservatoire; concerts in the church by the Bretton Woods Boys' Choir. The area honored the former studio of a leading artist of the onetime White Mountain school of painters.

Granted the complexity of the matter one would still have to recognize that the aesthetic life of the popular culture was anemic. Moreover, what holds true of the aesthetic taste of a society tends also to apply to its moral sensitivity. Aesthetic and moral tact are closely related, manners and morals. Even before Hollywood and television made their inroads on Main Street, the older New England excellencies had widely become enervated, whether as regards neighborliness or as regards the arts and ceremonies of the common life. Again with shining exceptions. As in other parts of the country the older decorums of the community could become censoriousness, and suspicion could take the place of neighborliness. It was this same New Hampshire which put Willard Uphaus in prison for a year for furthering international brotherhood in his community and refusing to expose his guests to prosecution.

Moralism and insensitivity with respect to the arts in those days was by no means confined to village and town. Heirs of the Reformation in city congregations and in our seminaries and colleges showed some of the same narrowness and austerity. The merged legacies of Puritanism and the Enlightenment in American culture forfeited their earlier vitality and came to terms with a pragmatic ethos. Much of our Protestant church life traced to the great visions and covenants of a once creative Calvinism. But where worldliness and Vanity Fair had then rightly been the enemy, now in a devitalized period there remained a great deal of anachronistic asceticism and inhibition.

To this day establishment Protestantism is inhibited and cramped with respect to the aesthetic and the sensuous. It is true that the Philistinism in the church is mainly due to the surrounding culture rather than to the religious tradition itself. But the theologian had long drawn a sharp line between God and the idols, between Spirit and flesh, between saint and worldling. And these once valid distinctions had become anachronistic in their applications.

In quite a different area we could document this lack of imagination in matters of faith in the period in question. Here it is a question of the approach to Scripture. After all the Bible is a panorama of visions and revelations. Granted that God speaks in it to the human heart and will, yet his persuasions are mediated through dynamic and dramatic language. Granted that he reveals himself in saving actions, it could only be by sacred recital invoking prophetic imagery that their import could be conveyed. Yet these oracles had come to be read and studied in wooden and denatured ways whether by liberal or evangelical. As has been well said, to submit the power of the prophets and the evangelists to the constraints of our critical methods is like trying to put lightning in a matchbox. But the rights of the Spirit and the imagination are equally frustrated when we try to turn such books as Daniel or Revelation into blueprints.

Biblical criticism has had its rights if only over against older and more recent forms of obscurantism. But such criticism has widely forgotten its original humanistic antecedents and inspiration from the days of Erasmus. In our own climate both rational criticism and biblicist literalism have reflected a common penury of imagination. It is not surprising that the secularist today neglects the Scripture or is led to some similarly wooden view of its bearing on modern issues. Fortunately the Bible today as in the past has its own ways of breaking through constraints. Not only Puritanism itself but such diverse movements as Mormonism or the Black church with its spirituals show that prodigies are possible when the dramatic mythology of the Bible comes alive.

Apart from such exceptions, the examples I have cited point to a basic insensitivity and inhibition with respect to the aesthetic order and the impulse to celebration. I repeat that it is a mistake to hold the Puritan tradition or Calvinism particularly responsible. The pragmatic temper of our whole society has more to do with it. If one looks for religious antecedents one should look not to our earlier Calvinist roots but to the consequences of the great revivals of the nineteenth century. Though this widespread movement encouraged emotional expression it channeled such emotion in intense but narrow syndromes which eclipsed all wider sensibilities.[2] The history of the revivals meant no less than a trauma in the American psyche, in Middle America, one whose effects still go on for better and worse both in our culture and in our religiosity. The awakenings and revivals represented momentous Christian renewal. But this kind of religious experience has had too narrow a focus. It blew

2. Cf. John B. Boles, *The Great Revivals: 1785–1805* (Lexington, Ky.: University Press of Kentucky, 1972), esp. pp. 192–95; Sydney E. Ahlstrom, *A Religious History of the American People* (New Haven, Conn.: Yale University Press, 1972), esp. chap. 29, and pp. 844, 1090. He speaks of "the radically individualistic accent of revivalism and its large role in extinguishing the Puritan's concern for the Holy Commonwealth as a whole." See also on the resulting sentimental context of Christian art, p. 745.

the minds of our populace as only an overwhelming experience of the sacred can do, and with consequent benefits. But the consequent conversionist patterns of renewal and vitality were individualist and in this phase anti-intellectual and antiaesthetic. Unfortunately this kind of regeneration—especially in the gilded age of expansion and affluence—played into the hands of the Philistinism of Main Street, the hick culture of the plains, the brash or brassy style of small town or suburb, the tastelessness of the religious arts, and the conformities and materialism of society generally. Reaction to it in this climate accounts for the mind-set of many home-grown positivists in our college faculties.

III

The place of the arts and the imagination in the religious life has passed through many vicissitudes in Protestantism. The ancient iconoclastic impulse in Christianity renews itself in new situations. Sometimes images and art-forms have been justifiably opposed not by moralism but by a more vital imagination in the church. The heirs of Milton and John Bunyan were properly censorious of the stage-plays of the Restoration. But too often the disparagement of the arts has been based on spiritual aridity and defensive conformity. Such attitudes have had a long history.

Charles Garside in his book, *Zwingli and the Arts*, quotes contemporary critics of the reformer who besides being a theologian was among the most accomplished musicians of his day. One such critic, Hans Salat, wrote: "Zwingli was practised in puerilities and frivolities, taught drum-beating, playing the lute, the harp, and was a complete musical pedant." Thomas Murner of Strassburg derided him as a "fiddler of the Holy Gospel and a lute player of the Old and New Testaments." Another called him "an evangelical piper."

But all this sounds strangely familiar. Where have we heard this before?

"We have piped to you and you did not dance." It is true that these words of Jesus occur in a parable. But the image of music-making referred to the Gospel, as against the work and mood of John the Baptist. Jesus was not a pagan Zorba the Greek, but music and dancing and the motif of the wedding feast recur in his words and ministry. At least his language danced, and one lame man whom he healed leaped if he did not actually dance.

Perhaps a theopoetic interlude may be allowed here.

If David was mocked for dancing
so David's greater son for piping.

If David played on the harp for Saul
  and eluded the javelin
Jesus provided wine for the wedding feast
  and was pierced by the lance.

When Jesus healed the lame, they didn't stop with walking,
  they danced.
When he healed the dumb, speaking was not enough,
  they sang.

The more easily to tumble
David and Francis cast off their garments.

If Jesus, called wine-bibber and friend of publicans,
was a Bohemian and a shaman
who taught chimeras and lived them out
until they took hold on the real;

So Paul was a jail-bird and a fantast
who acted out a new apocalypse
until it took hold on the real
and Rome became Europe,

a scene-changer and a world-changer,
an underground man with his guerilla troupe,
and a poster-artist
by whom Jesus Christ was "publicly placarded as crucified."[3]

This side-slip into one kind of theopoetic may suggest that the derision of Zwingli as an "evangelical piper" has had its parallels through a long history which, indeed, still continue.

IV

Appreciation of the arts in the churches has made much progress since the period I have been reviewing. Returning to the New Hampshire church which frowned on square dancing a generation ago I was astonished to find a tasteful and professional ballet group participating in the morning worship in the sanctuary itself. The General Conference of the United Methodist Church recently adopted a statement which among other things encourages "new forms of language, the writing of hymns and poems, productions in the visual and performing arts and multimedia presentations that seek to communicate authentic Christian truths." (But why "truths"? The artist does not seek to indoctrinate.)

In the meantime the program for demythologizing the New Testament did not help to clarify the relation of theology to the imagination. One misunderstanding of the plastic language of faith was called upon to correct the abuses of another. It is only when myths, fables, and poetry are taken literally that one is pushed to these expedients. Just because we lack imagination is no reason

3. Gal. 3:1.

to think that the ancients did. Just because their scenarios and world-plots were prescientific is no reason to impugn the primordial experience which shaped them.

Neoorthodoxy, for its part, also disparaged the imagination in favor of the will, the eye of vision in favor of the ear of obedience. It seemed to be thought that God or the Word could address us without taking account of how language works. The Reformers were all trained in the ancient humanistic art of rhetoric and knew that God persuades us through language that "moves" us ("*movere, delectare, docere*"). Luther called the Holy Spirit a "rhetorician." But neoorthodoxy and existentialist interpretation, though they appeal to the Reformers, exalt the Word and the kerygma apart from their media and imagery. It is not the human heart that is addressed but the will alone or some abstract core of freedom.

Today, however, the imagination is reasserting its rights. In the culture generally the children of Main Street rebel against the aridity and suffocation of the mores and appeal to phantasy. Students rebel against the "objective consciousness" both in the academy and in a technological society. The old pattern of utopian communities reappears. The revival tradition takes on a secular-charismatic form. More profoundly the new science and the new cosmology carry a shock to the sensibility of the West, disturb our deepest securities, and awaken the sense of wonder and imagination. The arts testify not only to the Age of Aquarius but to the Age of Apocalypse.

In this situation it is essential that theology and the religious institutions relate themselves to all these impulses, however ambiguous they may be. The language and liturgies of faith should respond to the new experience which also makes itself felt in many ways in our denominations and congregations. This means that we should be attentive to all those that speak out of this new revolution of consciousness. In exchanges with such men as Joseph Campbell, Norman O. Brown, James Hillman, William Irwin Thompson, and Alan Watts, with Rollo May and Mircea Eliade, we are properly dealing with religion at the level of symbolics and theopoetic. Theology, fortunately, already has a specialized corps dealing with Zen, Heidegger, Tolkien, and Hesse. We have our expert reporters on the literature of apocalypse and the new novel, on the avant-garde theater and on the graphic arts. We have our accredited representatives at Esalen.[4]

But all such exposure to the new powers and mythologies of our time should be furthered. The theologian with a long memory recognizes old patterns of gnosticism and intoxication in many of these contemporary dreams and cults. But he also recognizes that God is doing a new thing in our time. We see a renewal of the religious imagination all about us. Our eroded formulas must be quickened to match it as the new Word ripens.

4. On all such matters see the recent writings of Sam Keen, David L. Miller, Nathan A. Scott, Jr., as well as *Interpretation: The Poetry of Meaning*, ed. Stanley R. Hopper and David L. Miller (New York: Harcourt, Brace & World, 1967), and *Echoes of the Wordless "Word,"* ed. Daniel C. Noel (Missoula, Montana: American Academy of Religion, and Society of Biblical Literature, 1973).

5

Ecstasy, Imagination, and Insight

If, as many signs indicate, modern society is moving toward a new experience of depth and a new spirituality, there is one test that should concern us: the rich diversity of our Adamic makeup should be granted full play. It is on the earth and in the sunlight that our species works and plays, builds and fashions, orders the patterns of its families, tribes, and states. Our best dreams and myths relate to the many-sided faculties and talents of human nature in this theater of reality and action.

This test is met by contemporary mysticisms and cults so far as richer endowments than the cerebral are invoked. Openness to the powers of the soul provides a more dynamic sense of reality. But inwardness and its disciplines may also shortcut essential aspects of the human. If rationalism leads to vacuity so also can mysticism. The dramas of the psyche can leave the real world far behind, the good world of our five senses, our affections, our kinships and relationships, our skills and our talents. It is one distinction of Christian mysticism even in its most ecstatic exemplars that it gathers up all aspects and vitalities of our earthly creaturehood.

Some features of the new spirituality move toward this kind of plenitude: (1) a fresh naiveté, deliberately cultivated, vis-à-vis nature and natural forms, associated with an ecological mystique; (2) the new "wisdom of the body" with its heightened awareness of somatic existence and celebration, as in the dance; (3) interpersonal encounter but also communal exploration; (4) the zest and liberation associated with decommercialized skills, arts, crafts, farming, and other skilled occupations. Though these new creative thrusts often represent a revolt against conventional patterns yet they reflect in many ways a biblically grounded view of man and nature. But other current mystiques and mythologies forfeit much of the true human potential as did their gnostic or orgiastic or romantic precursors in the past.

Any plea for a valid theopoetic today must defend itself on two fronts. It must assert the rights of the imagination against abstraction, rationalism, and stereotype. But the enemy is also on the other side: the cult of the imagination for itself alone; vision, phantasy, ecstasy for their own sakes; creativity, spontaneity on their own, without roots, without tradition, without discipline.

The topic of ecstasy comes up in any discussion of theopoetic if only because religious experience and sacred texts have always been associated with inspiration. Another name for theology is divinity, and divine wisdom has always been thought of as imparted by the Spirit to those "in the Spirit."

No doubt there are different names for such afflatus. "I was in the Spirit on the Lord's day," writes the author of the Apocalypse when he was commanded to write an account of his visions. Wordsworth can speak of

> that blessed mood,
> In which the burthen of the mystery,
> In which the heavy and the weary weight

Of all this unintelligible world
Is lightened![1]

Modern poets and seers can speak of alterations of consciousness or of oneiric states, of openings, illuminations, and epiphanies, all associated with knowledge and power.

Those who are no longer at home with such categories as inspiration or transcendence, or such symbols as the Spirit, the soul, the muse, or the Word, still find ways of testifying to the dynamics of the self. They may speak of cosmic consciousness or blowing one's mind, or of some deeper awareness as of the tolling of Being or the Supreme Fiction or the Wordless Word. If there is no longer any supernal world above, speliologists of the Psyche can still excavate for echoes of Reality in the labyrinth beneath the cave beneath the cellar of our ordinary consciousness.

All such versions of secular initiation involve some kind of extranormal perception, some heightening or derangement of the senses, corresponding to what used to be called inspiration or possession. They also have their own techniques, inducements, and symbols.

But the cult of ecstasy today is compounded of so many confusions that true lovers of divine wisdom must mourn to see their concern travestied and given a bad name. What is perennially glorious about exalted human apprehension is muddied by every sort of kick or trip or contrived physiological intervention.

Much that I have to say about this area of contemporary religiosity will be negative. This does not mean that the scientific study of such matters is not valuable. All

1. "Lines composed a few miles above Tinturn Abbey," *The Poetical Works of William Wordsworth* (London: Oxford University Press, 1923), p. 206.

that we can learn about consciousness and its phenomenology, for example in connection with drugs or by way of anthropological observation, adds to our self-knowledge and can have its useful applications.

I

One can understand the current thirst for spiritual liberation in our society. We are heirs of a twofold tradition contributing to the stifling of the spirit and the emotions: on the one hand the sway of rationalism and on the other an inhibiting religious asceticism. It was inevitable that human nature would reassert the rights of spontaneity even in explosive ways. The low ceiling in our pragmatic age, the one-dimensional flatness of a life subject to the tyrannies of dwarfed expectations and responses: all this was bound to bring forth its reaction.

But the reaction and the release are conditioned by the givens of the situation. The rebels are still the children of a garish age, and their dreams are too often the mirror-image of their earlier limitations. Their cults and their phantasies have not extricated themselves from their home ground in Middletown, "Peoria," and Hollywood. The transcendent liberation of many, even when ticketed with the Orient, is still mired in Philistia. There are phantasies that are self-flattering and visions that are synthetic. There are euphorias and ecstasies, but it is a question of whether they have been earned.

The children of Main Street are neither Ariels nor Calibans but hybrids of both. Why should they think that their seizures and illuminations are either interesting or trustworthy? Even our more sophisticated initiates, tutored in all the arcane lore of our Alexandrian age, are far from being either angelic or seraphic doctors. Their dreams, koans, and mandalas are conditioned by an unpropitious setting. Times like ours have brought forth their Peregrinus, their Nostradamus, their Paracelsus. It appears that we shall have to wait for either a Joan of Arc or a Pascal, a George Fox or a von Huegel.

In these situations of cultural ferment and prophecy, our forebears learned over and over again that the spirits must be tested. Enthusiasm is an old story. Especially in the Christian church these lessons should long ago have been learned. The issues were lived through in the church at Corinth in the first century. Paul, while glorying in the iconoclastic Spirit, makes clear that the "flesh" has its own intoxications—meaning not sensuality but unpurged Eros in all its aspects. In the early sixteenth century the eroding of spiritual and cultural order again brought forth a period of creative and destructive antinomianism with its riot of visionary romanticisms calling for discrimination. In the American scene Jonathan Edwards' dissection of heavenly and morbid impulses in the *Great Awakening*—recently gathered together and published in the Yale Jonathan Edwards series—stands as a paradigm of American religiosity.

Again, today, we are confronted with ambiguous cults of ecstasy and Eros in both unsophisticated and sophisticated quarters. Their defenders often do not distinguish between ecstasy cultivated for its own sake and ecstasy as a by-product of a new insight achieved through struggle, whether of the scientist, the artist, or the saint.

Our emotional and instinctual makeup is a powerhouse. These dynamics can run free, gratuitously, like the driving belt in a factory when it is not engaged with its proper load. The ensuing dramatics of the psychic life are intense. One can manipulate the theater of our basic responses just as one can shake a toy kaleidoscope. The human constitution is such that we crave interest, excitement, drama, intensity. Special cultural conditions heighten this demand for relief from boredom or acedia. The seductions in question are all the more powerful because they are allied to normal plenitude of experience.

One should in fairness recognize that even questionable explorations of the occult and the irrational may have their value viewed as symptoms and auguries of a wider movement of renewal. So in the sixteenth-century church, historians can identify in the heretic, Thomas Müntzer, many of the traits of the "radical Reformation" at its best. So also Jacob Bronowski can credit Müntzer's contemporary, the alchemist and astrologer, Paracelsus, as a kind of proto-scientist. But the task of discrimination is still with us.

II

In canvassing all such issues I have specially in mind a discussion some years ago of creativity and states of consciousness in which ecstasy was a recurrent theme. This gathering was in a Manhattan penthouse and was one of a series of exchanges devoted to the "new sensibility" programmed by the Society for the Arts, Religion and Contemporary Culture. Under the chairmanship of Rollo May and led by Dr. Jean Houston of the Foundation for Mind Research in association with Professor Walter Clark of Andover Newton Theological School—a specialist in the psychology of religion and known for his studies of drugs in this connection—the small company included artists, theologians, and social scientists. If we wish today to identify valid forms of modern spirituality—

such as can commend themselves to the human concerns and to the various forms of expertise here represented—this particular forum was of special interest. Implicit in the colloquy was the larger task defined for our desacralized age as that of the "naming of the gods," a topic indeed to which the Society moved in its subsequent agenda.

The breadth of the discussion was evidenced in the readiness to recognize common features in the creativity of scientist, artist, and mystic. In all these areas insight is associated with heightened experience or visionary moments. Here Dr. Houston brought in her extensive acquaintance with the history of mysticism. A painter testified that his best work was accomplished not only in association with intensified awareness but that it was the autonomous product of a trance-state. This view of the work of art was supported by a composer. One participant who evidently believed that the Dionysiac rapture should be acted out rather than talked about interrupted the proceedings recurrently and gave the chairman some difficulty. Many of those present remembered the remarkable paintings by a schizophrenic patient shown and discussed at an earlier session, suggesting the close relation between hysteria, ecstasy, and creativity. Meanwhile familiar testimonies of great scientists were adduced attributing their breakthroughs in physics, biology, etc., to quasi-ecstatic insight. Walter Clark contributed from his expertise on the relation of drugs to mystical and religious phenomena.

The demurrers raised in the discussion were predictable. So far as the artist is concerned one meets the classic case of Paul Valéry insisting on the role of the poet as conscious craftsman. Jacques Maritain in his

Creative Intuition in Art and Poetry,[2] while according a large place to the subconscious and defending the surreal and the iconoclastic in modern art, nevertheless held to the Aristotelian-Thomist distinction, according to which the work of art is assigned to the practical reason rather than the contemplative or purely spiritual. One can add here the life-long disparagement by W. H. Auden of the artist as "magician," or one who works in spells and claims religious authority for art.

So far as the mystic is concerned the discussion pointed to the long struggle dating from both the Old Testament and from Plato between true inspiration and false, between reality and illusion. So far as the scientist is concerned there is the question as to whether the sudden flash of insight is not more related to his antecedent labors than to the ecstatic state that accompanies their resolution.

Jean Houston agreed that the insights and metamorphoses of the self associated with ecstasy are related to prior disciplines. I would suppose that neither Einstein's clarifying formula nor Dante's vision of the rose in the *Paradiso* were presented to them on a silver platter while they idled. No doubt meditation and a wise passivity and negative capability were involved, but also years of intense application. If this law holds for the genius it also holds for the rest of us. We cannot shortcut divine wisdom by manipulation, nor should we confuse psychic pyrotechnics with the fulfillments of a long period of gestation.

If it be granted that prior disciplines are the condition

2. Jacques Maritain, *Creative Intuition in Art and Poetry* (New York: New American Library, 1955), esp. chap. 2, "Art as a Virtue of the Practical Intellect."

of significant vision then it is a question of what kinds of discipline. Is it a question of special techniques of transpersonal awareness and manipulated alterations of consciousness? Or is it a question of the appropriate disciplines of scientist, artist, saint—or, in the case of any one of us, the disciplines of the heart? No doubt there are many kinds and degrees of self-transcendence, and this makes for a large part of the confusion.

Those who favor exotic regimens or one or another kind of shock procedures such as orgiastic initiations or ingestion of drugs may well argue that the tabus and mental habits and sterility of our culture necessitate them. After all even traditional Christian piety has assigned a place in its patterns or calendars for retreats, drastic self-inquisition, fastings, even flagellations, as well as revivalistic Pentecosts fostered by all manner of favoring stimuli. To put the matter in the most banal terms, however, it is always a question of quality, and this is determined by context and intention. In a given situation there can be healing in intoxication as there can be *in vino veritas*. But madness is not always sacred. The powers of the soul can be dangerous. The daimonic may turn to the demonic.

Anyone who studies the history of religions soon learns that ecstasy is one of their most ordinary and omnipresent features. Frenzy and trance naturally evoke awe so that there soon develop techniques for inducing them, and the state becomes associated with religious authority. But ecstasy is basically a physiological condition akin to anesthesia. In some social groups there is what is called a low threshold; that is, members of the group require little stimulus to pass into a trance state. With other groups or individuals there is a high threshold. But it is a physiological matter, no doubt with psychic accompaniments, and in itself has no cognitive, aesthetic, or spiritual significance. This is clearest in the case of epilepsy. Epileptics report blissful split-second phases of their attacks, as would accord with a state of anesthesia. Dostoievsky describes his own epilepsy in *The Idiot.* Prince Mishkin who speaks for him here emphasizes the ambiguity of any supposed revelations.

Joseph Klausner, a leading authority on early Christianity, attributed St. Paul's visions to epilepsy and thus sought to explain the heretical features of his Judaism. As well attribute Paul's originality to his bow legs as described in a late apocryphal writing. Common to all forms of ecstasy is a basic psycho-physical mechanism and this is of no more special interest than any involuntary sequence in the body such as the relation of fear to adrenalin. The ecstasy of a St. Francis and the trance of a medium have a common organic basis and one must look beyond this for any special significance. The supersession of normal consciousness may, indeed, be valued as liberating where boredom prevails. It may be sought as novel, forbidden, or exciting. But then for any real importance all depends on the ingredients of the transaction.

It may be argued that ecstatic experience in itself has at least the value of awaking the subject to a transsecular, a spiritual, sense of existence. But what a low level of spirituality is this: how gratuitous, subjective, and inconsequent. It is like the spirituality or faith induced by parlor seances or E.S.P. Where transformation of consciousness occurs in the counter-culture, whether through practises of meditation or through drugs, resulting in significant enrichment, one can be sure that other factors are operative: at least indirect influence of some great cultural or moral tradition.

One is reminded here of Austin Farrer's insistence in his *Rebirth of Images* that the idea of a pure, naked spirituality is a chimera, a non-sense. In other words an ecstatic moment, a creative apprehension, always has a context. It is a mistake, he writes, to suppose that "spirituality came naked into the world, or could exist without the images that condition it." But then the images and the life-attitude they presuppose count for everything in the quality of the experience. I recognize that there is a school today which makes it a program to go deeper than any symbol, to emptiness or nonbeing. But images return through the backdoor.

III

What I have said so far about extranormal states of consciousness may seem mainly negative. But my caveats have been directed against misunderstandings and abuses. It is not a question of quenching the Spirit or failing to recognize the never fully explored dynamics of the self. The very idea of a theopoetic or a mythopoetic presupposes dimensions of awareness associated with vision. Evidence or documentation from any quarter bearing on mankind's ultimate transactions with the gods or the mysteries are to be cherished and related to one another.

All such can be welcomed if it be agreed that what is important is not the particular state of consciousness or its mechanics but the quality of what is mediated. Perhaps for some vegetablelike existences the sole fact of passing over their low threshold into a state of possession, euphoria, or convulsions constitutes supernal knowledge. If a person is knocked on the head and sees stars he might as well make a claim to cosmic consciousness. Under the influence of black coffee and brandy at midnight sophomores have become Platos and Shakespeares and have been granted the ultimate secrets of the universe —but in the morning their scribblings were no such matter. Artists and mystics have first to practise their scales and learn their a, b, c's and train their reactions. Inebriation is no substitute for paidcia.

Yet it is true that all our best illuminations and creativity are associated with intensity of experience. No doubt consciousness "alters" in any case through a wide gamut all the time, but sometimes with a more burning focus. Here it may be difficult to distinguish between absorption, mood, "brown study," fascination, afflatus, the waking dream, transport, ecstasy. The category of ecstasy itself can refer either to beatitude or to trance proper.

The heart of the matter is the state of absorption and intense focus of attention. Here the imagination is autonomously active of itself, whence the acute gratification. For it involves the ordering of experience, the shaping of confusion, the crystalization of ambiguity, the discharge of a burden. All this holds for mystic, artist, or scientist. It holds for all of us. Both knowledge and power are the upshot, both insight and liberation. But the affective aspects which may run from tension and excitement to elation and rapture are not be separated from the creative process or sought for themselves.

The contemporary widespread exploration of meditation and mysticism can help to shape a Christian theopoetic for our time. This hunger for reality in the West is the symptom of a profound gestation going on in a society in which spontaneity has been blocked. We see in many quarters a renewal of the imagination taking both orgiastic and sophisticated forms. Christian experience, symbol, liturgy, and theology itself can be nourished by it. So far as a new secular awareness and mentality demand their own expression this must be incorporated in the task. Older Christian models should be open to the new constellation of factors.

IV

In discussions of ecstatic phenomena today such as the one I mentioned above insufficient attention is paid to biblical and Christian examples. Evidence is cited from esoteric sources, from Eastern practise, from the use of drugs. If the Christian saints are mentioned it is only in relation to the more sensational features of their testimony. The interest is in psycho-somatic mysteries and techniques of transcendence rather than in the human and moral ramifications of such states and visions. The use of drugs is even assigned to Jesus and his first followers as though no powerful spirituality in history could be explained apart from the mushroom.

If I may be pardoned a personal observation, I have sometimes been nettled that our contemporary initiates and cultists should think that they alone know about human potential and higher planes of consciousness. The turned-on and the consciousness-raisers think that they have discovered something or recovered something from remote or hidden lore unknown to the rest of us. Even in the churches, Pentecostalists should not think that they are the only ones who know what it is to be in the Spirit. One is sometimes tempted oneself, after the reluctant fashion of St. Paul, to boast of visions and revelations and of being taken up to the third heaven, or to tell of retreats at Assisi and other sacred precincts, or a pilgrimage to the Buddhist shrines at Mihintale. I have sat with James Luther Adams through discussions of blowing one's mind, and no one thought to ask him about his retreats and spiritual direction with the Benedictines at Maria Lach before many of them were born.

Many of our generation like Adams and Douglas Steere were thus early initiated into the influence of such figures as Friedrich von Huegel, Evelyn Underhill, and William Orchard, and to such hearths of the religious life as Iona, Talbot House ("Toc H"), and the French Catholic revival associated with Charles Péguy and focusing on Chartres, and into personal associations with such men as Albert Schweitzer, Rudolph Otto, William Temple, and Rufus Jones. We may be pardoned for pressing the question of credentials on the oracles of a new generation.

Of course in those days there were also the Rudolf Steiners, Keyserlings, Blavatskys, and Gurdjieffs. Differing climates produce differing explorations "beyond the threshold." In their cases, valid protests, curiosities, and hungers were entangled with outworn magical ideas and preposterous mythologies. Even the hard-headed English were infiltrated with Celtic dreamers, mediums, and table-tippers. Rudolf Steiner turned the Gospel of John into a book of theosophic pantheism, but his romanticism had its valuable impact on pedagogy. The poetry of Yeats, like a blossoming clematis, found a useful lattice work in the arcane cosmology of Blavatsky. G. R. S. Mead and the group that published the *Quest* two generations ago in London made important contributions to the history of ancient Gnosticism. So today there are baffling issues to be sorted out in the esoteric and charismatic movements of the time.

In this country Irving Babbitt, according to James Luther Adams, liked to quote Bossuet's remark that so much evil had issued from what calls itself mysticism that it is an appropriate policy to oppose it all. Without going so far the Christian may well recall the theme in T. S. Eliot's "East Coker" that we must often "wait without ecstasy," that ecstasy comes only after the agony of death and rebirth, that

> in order to arrive there . . .
> You must go by a way wherein there is no ecstasy.[3]

My personal reminiscences are only to suggest that our own Western Christian tradition down to the recent past offers both resources and criteria for consciousness-changing. Those avid today for transpersonal awareness might be surprised to know what beatitude could be experienced in the old-fashioned prayer meeting in many churches. Or in dedication services at student conferences. Or at hill-top meditations such as those led by Howard Thurman or Robert Calhoun at sunrise in the old days for the Hazen and Kent conferences. On such occasions charismatic leadership, the setting, the silence, the responsible concerns of all present, all these favored ineffable unveilings. But such experiences came naturally. They might be favored by this or that liturgical medium, or by the promptings of song or image. But such incitements all entered in as ingredients of a gestation whose main import was not seizure but purgation and orientation to the personal or common task.

3. T. S. Eliot, "East Coker," *Four Quartets* (New York: Harcourt Brace, 1943), p. 15. Reprinted by permission.

Here is the test: What quality or scope of the inner life, what human or moral ramifications, are involved and at stake in a given vision or dream-state? What conflicts and of what outreach are resolved? What relation does the supranormal experience have to the actualities of life before and after?

In the New Testament we have a good test case because it appears to speak both for and against ecstasy. The author of the Book of Revelation, as already noted, tells us that he "was in the Spirit on the Lord's day," when his disclosures began, surely to be understood as an ecstatic state. Paul, though he bids his readers not to quench the Spirit yet discounts heavily ecstatic experience and language. Though Jesus was a charismatic, yet there is no evidence for his use of any special techniques for the cultivation of trances and visions. The "theopoesis" or dramatic imagination of the New Testament writings arise out of hierophany and vision. Its more discursive aspects of teachings and ethic rest on these dynamics. But there is no ecstasy for its own sake.

In his *A Rebirth of Images*, Austin Farrer discusses early Christian rapture as represented by the account of Pentecost. Here was a period "of great ferment and profound disturbance." The ecstasy was related to the "travail" in which through the Spirit the community reordered its older pool of images so as to make place for a new datum, its experience of Christ. That momentous process in which the social imagination of the group fused its earlier Jewish life-symbol into a new revelatory pattern was understandably signalled by visionary intensity.

Subsequent overemphasis on the ecstatic aspects, as Farrer shows, was often motivated by imitation, and so to this day. Ecstasy can be induced, together with its particular manifestations. He cites the case of the stigmata of Francis of Assisi. "It is uninteresting that mystics nowadays produce by meditation the appearance of the wounds of Christ on their bodies, because they know it may happen." But the same applies to speaking with tongues and other arresting phenomena, dictated by social suggestion.

The seer of the Apocalypse may be taken as another test case. There are scholars who believe that the visionary state he claims is only a convention of the apocalyptic genre. This is in part true. But John was certainly the vessel of several hierophanies, and the enhanced apprehension was inseparable from them.[4] Yet the important thing was not the subjective state but the revelation: insights crystalizing out of his own life history and the history of his community. John's vision and his great poem, as with any great poem, were prepared in his own travail. This preparation consisted in the fact that he was in a concentration camp on the island of Patmos because of his efforts for the Gospel. As he says, he was sharing in the tribulation and the kingdom and the endurance of Jesus. My point is that the state of ecstasy was a by-product and accompaniment of the deeper process of clarification. Visions, poetry, and wisdom are not so cheap that they can be secured by the shortcut of ravishment or intoxication.

4. Aage Bentzen agrees with Bousset that the visions of the apocalyptists "are not only forms" and that, for example, "real experiences lie behind the visions of 4 Ezra" (*Introduction to the Old Testament* [Copenhagen: G. E. C. Gad, 1952], I:257–58). Lars Hartman in his *Prophecy Interpreted* ([Lund, Sweden: C. W. K. Gleerup, 1966], p. 105) observes that "an author who uses well-established, conventional literary forms for rendering visions may nevertheless cast his own visionary experiences in precisely those forms which he has taken over."

6

Theopoetic and Mythopoetic

I

To explore the role of the imagination in theology and faith brings up all the baffling issues concerning myth, mythology, and mythical thinking. One cannot plead for a theopoetic without also defending a mythopoetic. One would like to turn aside from this topic since the definitions and discussions of myth have become so complicated and wearisome. But something very important is at stake here. For our purposes we can select the issues that concern us and try to use some fresh language and current discussion.

One can suggest the wide gamut of disagreements and confusions about this topic by the following series of capsule theses, related to definitions both popular and scientific: (1) Myths belong to an outworn mentality and have no meaning for us. (2) Myths are unfortunately still powerful and block a more humane outlook and more humane social patterns. (3) Primordial myths and archetypes constitute the enduring psychic order and orientation of the race. (4) Myths provide the structure of identity and cohesion of particular human groups and ways of life, and are therefore in perpetual conflict with one another. (5) New myths are arising all the time out of new changes in the human situation. (6) By demythologizing, the persisting truth of myth can be identified and reappropriated, as by existential interpretation. (7) Archaic myths can be repossessed even in a rationalistic age by a second level of naiveté (Ricoeur). (8) If the spirits are to be "tested" so are social dreams and myths which can project man's morbidity as well as his health.

In any case there seems to be a deep impulse in human nature to orient itself in the unknown by pictorial representations, by imaginative dramatizations and narratives. The metaphor, the fable, and the myth represent a kind of preliminary science, but they are more than science since in them intellect is only part of the knowing. The prior question is as to whether we admit this more total kind of apprehension as essential, whatever role we assign to a more critical rationality. We should not forget that imagination has its own reality-sense and its own tests of coherence. Lévi-Strauss has shown that the "savage mind," for all its naiveté and "prerational mentality" has its own kind of empiricism, lucidity, and rigor in dealing with experience. The same is true of the child, the poet, and the artist, however much they may also delight in the gratuitous play of the spirit. Yet beyond the plastic world-making of seer and poet it is true that we face the problem of what to do with those imaginative structures of the past which seem alien today.

Human consciousness projects itself. It is dynamic and daimonic. Its excess—like the imagination of the child—cannot be content with immediate appearance and actuality but transfigures these and moves in new geographies. As a listener becomes aware of higher and deeper octaves, so more generally man-in-the-world takes possession of ever richer and more subtle registers of existence and maps them as best he can.

No one is going to stop human nature from its impulse to shape the mystery that lies about us. Thank the powers that be that we can dream in this sense, that we can send out feelers in the unknown and fly colored kites into the azure or the storm. It is as natural to fabulate as to breathe, and as necessary. Figuration is not confined to bards and painters. The human heart would suffocate if it were restricted to logic. Even poetry is not enough if it stops short of the grander scenarios. Only so do we feel out the hidden structures of our being and draw down lightning from the skies. As for the older and even archaic dreams and chartings, the family of man is one and there are no oracles that are not still part of our wisdom.

To give immediate point to my plea I note two claims made today. One is that for the modern mentality myth is dead. This refers first of all to ancient myths but also to any similar kind of fictions or world-mappings that violate our secularized sense of a one-level empirical reality. Within that horizontal world, allegedly the only one, creativity is still possible; indeed, it is supposedly all the more genuine for having been liberated from otherworldly tyrannies. The imagination is allowed its free aesthetic or psychological play, its flashes of insight, its parables, koans, and fables. But on this view we deny ourselves any more total poiesis. We do not aspire to put the world together.

There is one misunderstanding about this view of secularism. It is true that dualistic categories are increasingly unreal to the modern consciousness. For us the realities associated with older two-story myths and conceptions need to be appropriated in terms of our own experience and sensibility. But this does not mean that those realities cease to exist. Myths and categories of transcendence can still be eloquent for us if we awaken to the power that shaped them. We should not confuse the sometimes dated categories of older myths and epics with their essential vision.

Another related claim often heard today is that the Christian Gospel should be extricated from its mythological legacies. In our empirical age the theologian as well as the preacher should confine himself to a secular idiom. The working of the Spirit is to be located in our human and actual reality, and this excludes supernatural levels and language. The redemptive operations of God can be most cogently conveyed not by unreal heavenly scenarios but by mundane similitudes and challenges, by aphorisms and paradoxes that shock our assumptions and transform our outlook.

Thus we hear in some circles the order of the day: "from myth to parable." Back to the earliest speech of Galilee. We should return from the supernatural and apocalyptic imaginings of the apostles to the earthly aphorisms and comparisons of Jesus, especially to the nonmythological parables. This characteristic form of his teaching is secular through and through, yet conveys both his radical summons and his hope. If orthodoxy is concerned for the doctrine of God's incarnation in the flesh and in our daily life, where is the end-result more powerfully evident than in the homespun parables? These metaphors and stories are as eloquent and negotiable in the twentieth century as in the first.

This persuasive thesis takes various forms among New Testament scholars today. The study of the parables has taken a leading place among those concerned with the historical Jesus and with New Testament theology. Embarrassment with the mythological categories of the Gospels had led influential interpreters like Ernst Fuchs in Germany to an existentialist approach to Jesus and his sayings. In this light it is above all in the parables that not only his teaching but his purpose, action, and the mystery of his person are disclosed. In this country scholars like Dan Via, Robert Funk, and Dominic Crossan have agreed with him, but have rightly insisted on the literary, rhetorical, and structural traits of the parables as crucial in their communication. This extensive exploration of the parable-genre has immensely quickened our sense of their original import and continuing resonance.

But this whole approach to Jesus' teaching by-passes too quickly the wider symbolic or mythic elements which he inherited and employed. His parables alone, even with the life of action which framed them, would have been ambiguous without the prior mythical horizon of the kingdom of God as he announced it, so also evoking the basic orientation of his people. The "secular" parable was, indeed, deeply evocative and fate-laden for the hearer, but it was only one strand in Jesus' teaching. If the cosmic symbol he also employed is anachronistic for us—and that is still in some respects an open question—at least some such larger world-representation and time-representation is proper to the biblical faith in any age. Today, without this wider vision and sanction, even the parables and "the Jesus of the parables" offer us only a diminished perspective.[1]

1. No one has done more searching work on the parables of Jesus recently from the point of view of their language, shape, and structure than John Dominic Crossan. (See his *In Parables: The Challenge of the Historical Jesus* [New York: Harper & Row, 1973].) One of his findings, however, would seem to illustrate this insufficiency. It is that Jesus by the paradox and scandal in his stories was concerned to shock existing ways of thinking and by confounding habitual expectations and categories to awaken his hearers to the dimension of the unthinkable and the order of the miraculum. Indeed this was the role of Jesus himself. Thus his parables are like Zen koans and the paradoxes of Kafka. Such a view is congenial to our contemporary iconoclastic mysticism and thirst for the Absolute, but it disengages Jesus too radically from his home soil and the faith of his fathers. Jesus' mythos of the kingdom of God has more content in it than this kind of ontological reversal.

We should not let the culturally conditioned changes in our categories for the transcendent block our recognition of the reality itself or deprive us of the disclosures of its nature that have entered so deeply into the best life of mankind.

II

Granted all the inconclusive debates of specialists about myth and mythology, no one can deny the persisting power of the social imagination of mankind, past and present. Epochs have their dreams and world scenarios governing their arts, language, and politics. This remains true in our own disordered time. Mankind has its dreams and fables, and "dwells poetically on the earth." Before and behind all logics and techne lies his primordial plastic dealing with the world. Modern poets, as we shall see, find even archaic myths emerging in power and reenacting themselves in their experience and writing.

But here, as with poetry and the imagination generally, we meet with blocks and confusions in the modern mind which undercut any proper appreciation. Those same hard-headed rationalists and pragmatists who say that myth is dead have their own myths without knowing it. They think they are objective, dispassionate, and masters of their own thought. In this complacency, they remind us of the individual who claimed to be a self-made man, "thus relieving the Creator of a great responsibility."

Our myths whether recognized or not are what animate us and direct us: they face us this way or that; they open and close our horizons. The myths of a society or a class or a tradition can orient or disorient, animate or impoverish, bless or confound. Even the scientific humanist has his myth, the supposition about the world that like a lens focuses and limits what he sees. I have cited the case of Joseph Bronowski who sees the "ascent of man" in terms of his flexible adaptation and his empirical and rational dealing with experience. This author, as I have noted, is somewhat embarrassed by the great religious founders and other visionaries but manages to include them on his side as humanists and liberators. The future is secure if obscurantism can be left behind. For all that is valid and engaging in Bronowski's rehearsal of human creativeness and accomplishment much is left out of this focus. Yet who can doubt that such a scientist had his myth, his vision, and his metaphysics, and that they were related to his own notable achievement?

Yet it is to be granted that all this begs the question as to what we mean by myth. One can at least begin by thinking of it in terms of social imagination and its myths and scenarios. I only insist that these involve the will as well as the dream. Our visions, stories, and utopias are not only aesthetic: they engage us. They also represent some kind of knowing as well as fancying. Myths, dreams, and imaginations are serious.

It would indeed be well if we could find another term than "myth" for what concerns us here. It is perfectly understandable that to many it suggests superstitions and fanciful fictions. The common sense or reality sense of men has always rightly disparaged the weaving of fantastic tales about the gods and supramundane mysteries. But the term has this kind of ambiguous history. In the New Testament itself we find the Greek word *mythos* only five times and always in the sense of "silly myths" and "old wives' tales." Yet the New Testament is full of mythopoesis, of mythical dramatizations of the course of the world. Meanwhile from the time of Plato on the term itself has had an honored sense in the West associated with imaginative wisdom. Modern social science insists on the essential role of mythology in sustaining human communities.

For our purposes, therefore, we should move beyond the equation of myth and falsehood. We should also move beyond the version of this view in the Age of Reason which disparaged myth as only a dressing up of an idea in narrative, to be set over against factual or rational reporting. This view undercuts not only myth but all symbolic statement.

In a time like ours one must argue not only against those no-nonsense or cerebral types who identify the imagination with fancy. One must also awaken those who live an impoverished dream-life to the true dynamics of the spirit and to those impulses and poetries of the heart which orient us in the unknown. If there are those who object to myth on grounds as they think of intellectual honesty there are more who disqualify it because of their own debility and spiritual undernourishment.

But then comes the question of criteria among those who fully recognize the role of the imaginative and myth-making impulse. In every age the war of myths goes on determining both the disorders and the vitality of a society. We must always seek those ultimate world-pictures and stories which best answer to the total experience of mankind.

In our situation a special feature is present. Many seek the life of the imagination passionately but draw back from any encompassing myth. The experience of transcendence is craved but no larger plot or world-story is hoped for. They cultivate aesthetic or mystical initiation but are "against interpretation." At most they acknowledge a polytheism of fragmentary insights and look for no unifying pattern. One can illustrate by the medium of music. The religion of hosts of men and women of our age, the rare supreme moments of their years, are associated with the wordless and ineffable sacraments of the concert hall and the record-player, raptures so well suggested in the great pages of Proust on this art. But analogies are found in all aesthetic experience.

But true myth, involving language as it does, goes beyond any such momentary epiphanies and seizures, and pretends to order both experience and reality. In any case the arts of speech and language—epic, drama, poetry, the novel—raise the question of meaning in a more explicit way than is possible with music, dance, architecture, painting. The poet today may, indeed, use only broken myth, may use the great myths of the past in only derivative ways, but since he uses language his work can hardly escape some sort of defining statement. Poets have never been able to turn poetry completely into music.

By way of anticipation I would only ask the reader to keep his mind open to the momentous world-making role of particular visionary milestones in the human story. It is a question of doing justice to that mysterious potential in the human spirit whose transactions with reality have established clues or charts or ordering symbols far above our ordinary wisdom or nescience—revelations not only from "above" but emerging from the creaturely wrestle with circumstance.

These patterns of meaning were crystalized at junctures of the human pilgrimage more propitious to ultimate disclosures than our own situation and we do well to attend upon their wisdom. As with the individual so with a whole society or age, there are moments when the meaning of life is suddenly disclosed in depth, and these glimpses govern all other illuminations. Tolstoi well illustrates this truth as it concerns the individual in the case of Anna Karenina. At the moment of her suicide under the wheels of the train the whole meaning of her life, beyond her apprehension hitherto, was revealed to her in a flash of far-reaching illumination.

Those who bore for water or who mine for silver or gold select a promising site for their operations. In some terrains the water level may be very deep or seasonal or nonexistent. In many regions there are no mineral lodes. Many suppose that our moment in history, our modern categories, apperceptions, and horizons, are as propitious for divination and ultimate disclosures as other epochs. This kind of provincialism in time leads us to absorption in our own level of vision. But it is at other conjunctions in the story of cultures that the gods have spoken most clearly and that the deeps have been revealed.

This is not to say that in our present some grasp in depth of the dynamics of the world is not a continuing task. But it should be carried out with due reverence for the disclosures reported from more crucial occasions. The highly sophisticated dissection today of the psyche and its dreams by Jungians, mythographers, and oneiroscopes has its value in recognizing the prerational structures of consciousness and its symbols. But like a laboratory experiment, all such explorations are predetermined by the approach and the assumptions. What if major factors and givens are excluded in the procedure? Our age may be knowledgable about limited mechanics of the self, perhaps chiefly as "driven by daemonic, chthonic powers." But as T. S. Eliot writes in *Four Quartets*:[2]

2. T. S. Eliot, "The Dry Salvages," *Four Quartets* (New York: Harcourt Brace, 1943), p. 27. Reprinted by permission.

To communicate with Mars, converse with spirits,
To report the behaviour of the sea monster,
Describe the horoscope, haruspicate or scry . . .
or dissect
The recurrent image in pre-conscious terrors—
To explore the womb, or tomb, or dreams; all these are usual
Pastimes and drugs . . .

Beyond the curiosities of this "dimension" are greater mysteries and greater liberations. The twentieth century may have its epiphanies but it is not a favorable time for the greater visions and wider circumspections. Its intellectuals especially are out of their depth in dealing with those dimensions of experience for which earlier epochs have found a language.

These considerations lead to two further caveats with respect to the mythical legacies of the past. For one thing we should not too quickly accept the view of a discontinuity between the archaic mythic mentality and the modern mind. It is true that "primitive" tribes and early man are said to experience their total world as an unbroken dreamlike reality. They lived the myth from within. To move from the mimetic and magical realism of the Dionysian cult in the archaic phase to the Bacchi of Euripides is already to take on the role of observer so that the original obsession of the myth is broken. But the power of the myth and its authentic roots in abiding aspects of human being were not broken, nor are they to this day. Deep-seated myths of the past can have a relation to the human psyche and culture and language like that of Euclid to human reason.

A second caveat has to do with our misunderstanding of the kind of statement represented by a myth. In saying as many do that a given myth is obsolete or inaccessible to us because it assumes, say, a Ptolemaic cosmology or supernatural beings or a particular view of time (in this case as charged against early Christian eschatology), we are taking a very superficial view of it. These aspects, unacceptable to our conceptual habits or even to our cultural-symbolic conventions, are not the heart of the myth. Its depth can operate through all such time-conditioned features to enact itself ever anew in the unchanging continuities of human response and motivation.

This is not to deny that myths do in their own way map reality and involve particular views of such categories as time, space, and causation. Myths of any significance have a noetic or cognitive component just as the imagination is more than fancy. Aspects of the world as it really is report themselves in the myth, all the more primordially as the prophetic occasion that evokes them is more crucial. Myths of the fall tell us something more than arbitrary about the history and the conditions of human life in the world. The myth of Prometheus carries instruction with respect to man's dealing with nature and its costs. But whatever cognitive orientation a myth communicates is to be grasped by the same kind of imaginative apprehension that first shaped it, and only then transposed provisionally into conceptual statement.

III

We can explore further the basic issues with respect to myth and theology by recalling a remarkable encounter of poets and theologians some years ago. This meeting in Washington under the auspices of the Church Society for College Work in October, 1967, dealt with "Myth in Religion and Literature." The direction taken by the papers and discussion is evident in the title of the published report as edited by Tony Stoneburner: *Parable, Myth and Language*.[3]

If it is a question of the viability and meaning of myth for the modern mind and for modern faith one could say that this was a summit meeting. The theologians present included James M. Robinson and Robert W. Funk, among the most influential figures in New Testament interpretation in this country. The poets included Robert Duncan and Denise Levertov, outstanding representatives of a major direction in contemporary poetry. John Crowe Ransom was detained but shared with us the outline of a paper on "The Poet's Religion." The sessions were chaired by Stephen Crites, and other participants included Hollis Summers, Philip Zabriskie, and Samuel Laeuchli, church historian, whose paper was on "Christianity and the Death of Myth."

What immediately arrested our attention was that the poets of course assumed and demonstrated the use of myth in their work while the theologians insisted on the death of myth today. Evidently they understood myth differently, but there were basic issues remaining. Here is Laeuchli speaking:

> Myth had been cosmic-poetic theology. It was a statement about life told as a story about gods; theology projected upon the screen of heaven. It created a vision of life. It gave whole cultures a frame in which they could think and play and in which their imagination could grow. Myth presupposed a poetic relationship between earth and a world above, an up-and-down that seemed to give direc-

3. Tony Stoneburner, ed., *Parable, Myth and Language*, National Institute for Campus Ministries, 885 Centre Street, Newton Centre, Mass., 02159 (1968), 73 pages. See also Tony Stoneburner's report on the meeting in *The Christian Century*, 10 January 1968.

> tion and security to man and his society; it created a static, enclosed globe with the safe heaven above and a safe earth on which history goes on.[4]

Evidently, he noted, the crisis of such myth in our modern age is a serious one. Laeuchli recognized the continuing need of poetry after myth has gone. "No age can exist without poetry, without imagination creating the song, the dance, the poetic vision of life. We need the drama in which we can identify and gaze at the mystery of man."[5] But as far as myth proper is concerned, with the passage of time the crisis of myth has become the death of myth.

> Who prays to Poseidon or Bellona? Who would make votive offerings to Astarte or Isis in order to find life? . . . To be sure, the death of myth is only one dimension of our life. People continue to go to Lourdes and the Ganges river. . . . [But] the myth is dead as a live option in contemporary creativity whereby the poet tells the story of gods as he copes with the problems of man. . . . The myth died because step by step, beginning with the Homeric epic, man pushed back the supernatural until he reckoned with the horizontal and with a new kind of space. . . . But what applies to the Greek myths has to apply to the Christian ones too, which is why the whole Christian church is in such an uproar today.[6]

In his paper Robert Funk elaborated "the theological repudiation of mythological language" with special reference to Rudolf Bultmann's program for demythologizing the New Testament. Bultmann "sensed the profound hold that literalism has upon the modern mind." He also

4. Stoneburner, *Parable, Myth and Language,* p. 8.
5. Ibid., p. 13.
6. Ibid., pp. 12, 13.

found justification in the fact that already in the earliest church such writers as Paul and John felt free to supersede the mythical language they had inherited, already subject to misinterpretation. Thus for communication to modern ears, tone-deaf to mythical vehicles, Bultmann sought to translate the Gospel into a language of direct personal address. Over against pictorial and imaginative persuasion he turned to a deeper level of existential encounter. Even simile, metaphor, and parable, adds Funk, were for him only "the decoration of language. In spite of his intense classical learning, he appears not to have a poetic bone in his body."[7] However this last remark should be understood as playful hyperbole. Whenever the great scholar preached in his Marburg parish church at the Christmas season he forgot all about his demythologizing and invoked the poetry of the birth narratives without any reserve.[8]

Evidently there is a difference between the crisis of myth and the death of myth. It is one thing to say that the mentality of the West has long passed beyond a great divide into a phase in which archaic mythological thinking and its stories are irrecoverable. It is another to say only that such apprehension is blocked in a literalist and rationalist culture.

Yet Robert Duncan urged in his paper that "wherever we open ourselves to myth it works to convert us and to enact itself anew in our lives."[9] And further:

> God strives in all Creation to come to Himself. The Gods men know are realizations of God. . . . And all mankind

7. Ibid., p. 62.
8. So Frau Bultmann in private conversation.
9. Stoneburner, *Parable, Myth and Language*, p. 41.

> share the oldest Gods as they share the oldest identities of the germinal cell. . . . But what I speak of here in the terms of a theology is a poetics. Back of each poet's concept of the poem is his concept of the meaning of form itself; and his concept of form in turn where it is serious at all arises from his concept of the nature of the universe. . . . A mythic cosmogony gives rise to the little world the poet as creator makes.[10]

Likewise Denise Levertov offered examples in her work of the ways in which ancient myth reenacted itself in her vision and in her writing. It was ironic that in the course of the discussion she could remark that "the poets in their peculiar way are believers and the theologians are skeptics."[11]

I would not suggest that Robinson and Funk were opposed to all theopoetic. Rather they discounted myth in the sense in which they understood it. Yet in his defense of it Duncan evidently had genuine archaic myth in mind. In any case Robert Funk began his paper in a most satisfactory way.

> The study of theology ought to begin these days with a study of poetry. This is not merely to hand a rose to the poets, but to advocate a sane program of theological rehabilitation, certainly of theological repatriation. Theology seems to have gone awhoring after the scientific fleshpots of Egypt. It has wandered so far afield that it has forgotten the wellsprings of its infancy. The antidote must be potent enough to restore sight to the blind and hearing to the deaf. Perhaps modern poetry is sufficiently strong medicine to enable the queen to shake off her torpor.[12]

10. Ibid., p. 39.
11. Ibid., p. 14.
12. Ibid., p. 57.

But evidently it is one thing for theology to enrich its apprehension by poetry and it is another for it to appeal to myth, even that of its own great legacy. The reason for this latter exclusion lay not only in the modern mentality but in the history of language itself. The meaning of such older stories as those involving the fall, redemption, judgment, and new creation is deeply buried and obscured behind older layers of language and thought-forms. Linked as they are with obsolete cosmology, with exploded categories of time, space, and causation, today they can only perplex and mislead.

One can find a good illustration of this difficulty in the brief communication contributed to the Washington meeting by John Crowe Ransom. His statement began:

> I. Although I do not myself accept all the Articles of the faith, I hope and believe that the Church will survive all its difficulties. It seems to me essential to all those persons who do not quibble over its Articles, but repair to the Church in order to be reminded ceaselessly of the Commandments.
>
> II. I am at least a Christian moralist, believing that Christ, with his Beatitudes and Parables and Sermons, was much the greatest moralist in human history. But I have a disaffection for the Doctrine of the Resurrection.

Again, accepting Kant's ideas of pure reason: God, freedom, and the resurrection, he adds, "I except the third." But evidently the block here for Ransom as for many is the mythological involvement of this article of faith. He can demythologize and retain others in Kantian categories but the resurrection of Christ is too massively implicated in ancient structures of thinking and imagination to come through. Even those who today accept it are widely misled as to its meaning. I shall return to this topic below and show how a secular poet, Delmore Schwartz, nevertheless magnificently reenacts the initial experience of the disciples and pierces through the ancient categories in which the event was reported.

Yet any such sovereign repossession of ancient oracles and their disclosures of the laws of the world is widely ruled out. Even if it appears to take place in the case of the uncritical worshiper at Lourdes or on the banks of the Ganges or in the church next door we suspect their version of the myth to be distorted or impoverished or anachronistic. Yet without the myth are we not even more impoverished? How long will the commandments prevail without the myth? And does not the myth have a life of its own so that it overcomes its own distortions, impoverishments, and anachronisms?

In the discussion in question, however, the theologians understandably felt constrained to speak for what we call the modern man and the modern sensibility. For vast numbers of men and women they could not, therefore, but question the use of biblical myth. This disqualification inevitably extended to classical myth. No doubt mythical motifs from Sophocles are invoked in modern psychology and from Homer in modern poets and dramatists. But this is not the same thing as a repristination of the mythical reality.

There was much discussion for example of Denise Levertov's poem, "The Prayer," about an experience at Delphi.[13] Against the charge that she as a modern could

13. The poem is in her volume, *O Taste and See* (New York: New Directions, 1962), p. 75. See her remarks about it in Stoneburner, *Parable, Myth and Language,* p. 27, and the discussion, pp. 31–32. Her paper at the meeting, "The Sense of Pilgrimage," has now been published in her book, *The Poet in the World* (New York: New Directions, 1973), pp. 62–86.

only be using literary allusion she insisted that the mythical world not of Apollo but of Dionysus had emerged to shape the poem, and indeed to set its mark on her later work. She found similar atavistic empowerment in poems of hers related to Aztec, Hassidic, and Welsh mythology. She could speak of "the dynamic experiencing of archetypal characters or actions."[14] Robert Duncan concurred.

IV

What such testimony of the poets should teach the Christian is that his own deeply buried theophanies and ordering symbols can emerge in power and reenact themselves in the present. Their power is such that they can overcome the dead letter of their tradition and the distortions of their intervening transmission. In Duncan's words again, "wherever we open ourselves to myth it works to convert us and to enact itself anew in our lives."

Of course when the myth comes to speech in a given poet it does so in terms of his or her own special sensibility and the special constellation of influences and circumstances that constitute his or her world. Similarly with the believer: the dynamic legacies of the faith renew themselves in him and through him in terms of his own conditioning. But there is continuity not only of the power of the myth but also of its wisdom: the light it throws upon this or that deeper aspect of existence.

It is here that contemporary theology and biblical interpretation often err. In seeking the immediate and powerful Word of God behind its symbols and myths—which have often indeed become literalized, obsolete, and imprisoning—they hope to clear the way for an unmediated encounter with God. This approach is called existential.

14. Stoneburner, *Parable, Myth and Language,* p. 21.

But God's revelations were mediated in images and mythos, and encounter was inseparable from a wider context of meaning. We underestimate the grace of God if we do not recognize that it blesses us not only with his presence and call but also with illumination of the ways of the world and his ways with it.

For the believer, therefore, "to open himself to the myth" it is not enough to open himself to the Word in some existential kerygmatic sense, but as Duncan says in his context, "to a store of human experience acknowledged in the language [of the myth] that gives whatever depth to my own experience."[15] The kerygma in itself as address and encounter is abstract and disembodied. It is supposed to represent God's grace and demand, engaging our freedom. But this is to reduce the mystery of revelation to the category of the will. The transactions between men and the gods are richer than that. They involve symbolics corresponding to man's many-sided grasp of experience and the social imaginations by which he has oriented himself in the world. In liturgy and festival, but also in prophecy, the divine reality mediates itself through plastic images and metaphors and stories which take hold of our experience. It is only through such a total register that the Gospel can reenact itself anew in any time.

But we must appreciate the objections of our theologians to this assertion of the perennial power of myth and the Christian mythological structures. Language and mental habits change. Old maps of reality based on different apperceptions seem quaint if not grotesque. When retained they subvert the original vision. One can illustrate by the Christmas story. The nativity texts and the

15. Ibid., p. 40.

advent festival as celebrated today widely betray or travesty the Gospel.

Yet the fault may not be in the myth or even in its categories but in the parameters of our hearing. The problem may not lie in the mutations of language but in the scale and compass of our responses, the quality of our answering imagination. Deep speaks to deep. The myth of the nativity, to call it that, has its own authentic and primordial truth and power. It can ever and again come to speech and renew itself in us by the action of the Spirit in ways that relate to new language-situations and in ways that correct inherited distortions.

When it is said that this is not possible because of the radical change in all our categories since the Ptolemaic age there is a basic confusion. There are levels of human mentality and imagery which change relatively rapidly. But there are deeper levels of consciousness and culture and language associated with momentous revelations in the earlier history of mankind in which continuity remains unbroken. It is not only that the modern reader can recognize a common human nature in the pages of Homer and Aeschylus, the Pentateuch and Job. More than that the poet can still find the god at Delphi, as Eliot's protagonist could become aware of "the third who always walks beside you" in "The Waste Land" (alluding to the Emmaus episode in Luke's account of the resurrection).

Our problem may be the crisis of myth but not the death of myth. And the crisis of myth may safely be left to the irresistible prodigality of the Spirit which ever and again empowers the imagination of an age and of the church, bringing forth things new and old. Meanwhile the Christian archetypes have by no means lost their power. The emancipated believer looks on the vitality of the Evangelicals and the sects and supposes that the hold there of the classical biblical imagination is only a survival doomed by the acids of modernity. But this is too easy an anwer. He might also ask himself about the undisturbed sway of the ancient visions for a wide public in the great oratorios, masses, and requiems of Bach, Mozart, and Verdi. Or the disguised but recurrent surfacing of the Christ-story or of other biblical motifs in the secular arts and literature, or of biblical archetypes in occasions of quickened political debate.

Individuals and societies may live for extended periods at a superficial level of pragmatic conscensus but their deeper life is open to buried dreams. When deep speaks to deep the incubus of mental habit is brushed aside and we become contemporaries of older visionaries. It has been noted lately that the mythical consciousness of the West, last fully exemplified in Vico, resumed its uninhibited sway after two hundred years in James Joyce, who appealed back to him. This means that in our culture many options are again open with respect to the spiritual legacies of the past, options that were narrowed by the mentality of the Enlightenment.

Joyce followed Vico in overcoming the tyranny of chronological time. This was possible because more important dimensions of existence invaded consciousness. Our ordinary coordinates of time and space associated with the clock and other measurements are useful for the business of life, but we can be overtaken by sudden visions and perspectives from the depths which posit other calendars and geographies. Painters register this conflict by surrealism and the writer presents scenes in which ghosts and revenants appear in the streets of the city, or in which ancient and modern epochs are merged. In an older writer like William Blake the world of the imagination inevitably had a dualistic character, as we see in his mythological works. But in our own century the conditions favor both a return of the myth and the coincidence of the mythical world with the everyday world. There are increasing elements in modern society which have the antennae for these developments.

These considerations have a bearing on any discussion of the role of myth in our time. With respect to the Christian legacy I have urged for example that the myth of the nativity has an autonomous, a self-activating life of its own springing from a dynamic archetype in our human constitution and related in its language to long vicissitudes of human aspiration. The myth of the divine child and the age of gold had both ancient roots and widely diffused versions in antiquity and has remained powerful to shape man's view of fate and the times and seasons. It is only by the myth that our celebrations of the return of spring or of the overthrow of tyrants take on universal overtones.

For another example we may take the kind of language employed by the early disciples in reporting the resurrection of Christ, a transaction always associated by them with the imminent renewal of the creation as a whole. (It was not a question of Jesus' deliverance from death as a separate miracle but of the advent of the promised kingdom of God.) This is, indeed, mythological language, though the myth of the resurrection itself is only part of a larger story of God's dealing with Israel and mankind. The transcendental categories and symbol in which the first Christians testified to the resurrection as sequel to, or as the other side of, the crucifixion reflected their visionary insights as conditioned by their inherited sensibility and mental categories. Their reports crystalized in somewhat varying narratives which like all true poiesis employed current genres and models and merged surrealist epiphany with earthy-historical actuality. We can also recognize polemic distortions in the form of evidential details which found their way into the testimonies in the course of argument with disbelievers. But the central mythological witness was meaningful to the answering imagination of many of that time and audience.

Despite anachronistic features the myth can still be meaningful to the answering imagination of a modern man or woman at the appropriate depth of response. But the meaning is blocked if the myth is not heard in the relevant imaginative context and apperception, if the drama is not seen in its proper lighting. In this context and at this level the myth and its symbolics have their own survival power.

For an example one can turn to Delmore Schwartz's poem, "Starlight like Intuition Pierced the Twelve," published in the *Kenyon Review* in the summer of 1944.[16] The author wrote me soon after that he considered this poem as perhaps the most important to him of any that he had then written. What is remarkable here is to find the total thrust of the resurrection myth transmuted into the language of today in the work of a modern secular poet.

If the myth itself were dead it could not so speak. If the Ptolemaic categories and alien mental habits of the original witnesses were a bar, the revelation could not come through. But what does come through is the living force of the original transaction itself, the world-metamor-

16. Later printed in *Selected Poems: Summer Knowledge* (New York: New Directions, 1959), pp. 238–40.

phosis celebrated in the Gospel story. Schwartz's poem is not built on mere literary allusion to the sacred texts, a common method of exploiting the mythological legacies of the world's classics. Nor are the moral and eschatological aspects of the resurrection surrendered in favor of some banal analogue of the seasonal renewal of nature. Here rather, to revert to the words of Robert Duncan, "wherever we open ourselves to myth it works to convert us and to enact itself anew in our lives."

In the poem the twelve disciples struggle with language to say how the world has ended and changed for them in the light of the glorified Nazarene and their helpless exposure to his brightness. Where the first-century testimonies naturally took on the form and genre of the epiphany-narrative common to ancient Israel and the Hellenistic world, Schwartz employs a variant of the modern "dramatic monologue." Where the early witnesses proclaimed cosmic renovation in the categories of apocalyptic, Schwartz evokes the "deep structure" of metamorphosis congenial to the modern imagination.

Among the testimonies of the disciples in the poem are the following:

"No matter what I do, he looks at it."

"No matter what is said, he measures it!"

"... That we
Saw goodness, as it is—*this* is the awe
And the abyss which we will not forget,
His story now the sky which holds all thought:
No matter what I think, think of it!"

"We have died once; this is a second life."

"My mind is spilled in moral chaos," one
Righteous as Job exclaimed, "now infinite
Suspicion of my heart stems what I will,
—No matter what I choose, he stares at it!"

"I must
Try what he tried: I saw the infinite
Who walked the lake and raised the hopeless dead:
No matter what the feat, he has accomplished it!"

"Unspeakable unnatural goodness is
Risen and shines, and never will ignore us;
He glows forever in all consciousness;
Forgiveness, love and hope possess the pit."[17]

It seems clear that the original event here again exerts its power to transform reality. Like Wordworth's traveler in the Alps the visionary is caught up in the enveloping spell of the myth. This example of its persisting operation would break down if the meaning of the resurrection were reported here in only psychological or mystical or even existential terms. But Schwartz's poem relays not only the psychic but also the moral, and not only the moral but the cosmic dimensions of the event. All essential elements of the initial revelation are at least implicit and have found a contemporary language and vehicle.

It is sometimes said that for our age the early Christian supernatural symbol must be remythologized rather than demythologized. But this suggests a transfer of the affirmation into the language of a different and supposedly more contemporary symbolic. Such is not the case in the present instance. Here, as in the acclamation of the first Easter, Jesus is risen and glorified; all "thought" is sub-

17. *Selected Poems,* pp. 238–40.

mitted to him and his story; and hell itself ("the pit") is harrowed. Thus the original myth asserts itself, and therewith the event that first called it forth.

It is true that while the poem does not represent a remythologizing of the Scripture it does modulate the original. It does not merely repeat it. We have here a good test case for the mutation of myth in various times and idioms. Persisting archetypes come to speech in different cultural situations by way of differing media, linguistic and plastic. Revelation relates itself to the hearer. But the resurrection story would be stultified if the horizons of world-drama were forfeited, that is, its Jewish apocalyptic structure. The resurrection had to do with the course and goal of the world-process, its throes and its consummation.

This full scope of the resurrection comes to speech in Schwartz's poem, communicated in a current genre with its colloquial diction and in a way related to our modern sense of reality—especially, as I have suggested, by invoking the motif of metamorphosis. This motif of magic transformation is one in which ancient categories of the supernatural can be made acceptable to the modern mentality. A universal feature of folklore and saga, it is congenial to the modern imagination as is evident in the arts of surrealism, the apocalyptic novel, and in the contemporary cinema. Examples are found in the work of Kafka and Ionesco, Cocteau and Bergman. For this kind of sensibility the accustomed world is not as fixed and secure as it seems but dynamic and fluid, as is human consciousness itself. Hence our openness to the possibilities of transformation. Here the modern imagination coincides with the early Christian apocalyptic imagination.

Schwartz's poem operates especially with one perennial

formula of metamorphosis: the viewer changed by what he beholds, or into the image of that upon which he gazes; the viewer transfigured or healed or blasted by what he looks upon. The fables of Medusa and the basilisk illustrate the archetype in pagan antiquity. In Scripture Moses sets up the brazen serpent in the wilderness so that the children of Israel can gaze on it and be healed. The Gospel of John finds an analogue here for the lifting up of the Son of man as a cynosure of salvation. The basic motif recurs in the *Divine Comedy* and in the stigmata of St. Francis. In Schwartz's poem the disciples look on the glorified Christ and he looks at them, and their total world is subverted.[18]

> "I looked too long at the sun; like too much light,
> Too much of goodness is a boomerang."
>
> "And we shall never be as once we were,
> This life will never be what once it was."

If it be said that this is only a poem, and that the Christian myth is only properly at home in the liturgical mysteries of the church, I note that a former student of mine arranged Delmore Schwartz's text for liturgical use and found it an authentic and moving vehicle for voices, choir, and responses in Christian worship.

18. For another example see Allen Tate's poem, "The Cross," in *Poems* (New York: Scribner, 1960), pp. 125–26.

Epilogue

I have noted that a theopoetic or plea for the religious imagination has to defend itself on two fronts.

It has to defend itself on the one hand against a pragmatic no-nonsense type of mentality, representing a kind of devastated area in a culture whose aesthetic and spiritual antennae have been blighted. In this camp are also rationalists and religious dogmatists for both of whom experience lacks its deeper creative registers. There are, indeed, genuinely vital religious groups today besides these which downgrade images and the symbolic order for their own reasons: thus many existentialists concerned with what they think of as a more immediate kind of encounter, or those mystics who would transcend images in the quest for an ecstatic emptiness.

On this front any plea for the religious imagination opens the critic to the charge of mere aestheticism. His concern appears to be fanciful or frivolous.

But the charge of aestheticism is all too often a defensive ploy to protect some conventional security or life-style. This tactic has a long history. As an analogy one can cite Ezekiel the image-maker. When he declaims his visions of judgment his hearers taunt him: "Then I said, 'Ah Lord God! they are saying of me, "Is he not a maker of allegories?" ' " (Ezek. 20:49). That is, "Look what a farceur! Is he not just a concocter of fables?" I take this as a parable. So too often the public deals with the poet, the churchman with the visionary, and the theologian with those attentive to the image-makers of the age.

But today our plea has to defend itself on another front. In the current resurgence of spirituality, mysticism, and phantasy it is necessary to raise caveats and to call for discrimination. Here the critic appears himself to be opposed to creativity and liberation, and is put down as a traditionalist.

It is true that in these chapters I have urged that contemporary quests should take more account of the spirituality of our biblical and Christian tradition. Dialogue here can be profitable on both sides. Recovery today of the sense of the sacred may well reject many aspects of the religious establishment, but this creative impulse may also nonetheless contribute to the quickening of traditional pieties and liturgies. Conversely, iconoclastic cults largely determined by today's special situation may well look to a deeper soil and an older experience when their first enthusiasm passes.

Granted that this book is written by a traditionalist as one first of all concerned for the renewal of the biblical tradition in our time, yet I have urged a very open and appreciative attitude toward contemporary secular quests. My position is that God is doing something new in our midst and that church and synagogue can ill afford to ignore it. History offers many examples of conjunctures in which the work of the Spirit and the surprises of grace have outrun the laggard frontiers of orthodoxy and institution. Settled habits in the faith have needed the shock and rebuke of uncanonical witnesses and of prophets in unexpected circles. Our period is just such a time.

Nevertheless the spirits are always to be tested. For our time as for all times the test has to do with the health, vitality, liberation of human life and its societies. Whatever creative impulses and illuminations we have to reckon with should relate themselves to actual human nature as it is constituted, to the faculties and activities of man determined by his place in nature, and his moral existence as a creature living in society and history. All this sets a question to any forms of spirituality which ignore these concrete aspects of selfhood and the full human repertoire.

By way of illustration I would suggest that many experiences of psychic depth and their lore are essentially thin and adventitious as compared with the richly human zest of a craft. Except those who have no musical initiation who would forego the infinite delight of a Mozart string quartet in favor of whatever solipsistic intoxication? Before cultivating a sixth sense we should be sure that we have made the most of our five senses. To carry the matter one step farther, what oneiric mysteries or disinterred secrets of consciousness nourish the indispensable incentives of the heart and the will to live compared with the vital social celebrations of tribe or people?

Spirituality and religiosity should develop out of man's empirical experience as *homo faber* and *homo politicus*.

All this points to the biblical vision of man with its strong sense of his somatic and historical involvement. The earthy humanism underlying Judaism and Christianity has of course its transcendental presupposition and superstructure. But these, including the horizon of eternal life, are not matters of esoteric vision, but corollaries of the initial robust grasp of man's being and potentiality.

So far, therefore, as these chapters have voiced reservations about contemporary secular mystiques and disciplines I have had one main point to urge. Whether they seek a deeper reality by way of transformations of consciousness, or a renewal of spontaneity and organic rhythms in play, dance, or even manic transport, or look for arcane wisdom and suppressed vitalities of the self in dreams, myths, and other archetypal disclosures, yet there is an order of reality, seemingly on the surface, that they may be in danger of forfeiting.

Granted that there are secrets, enigmas, echoes, and hauntings buried in the soul or on the margins of consciousness, are not these occult matters better explored through the known and the natural?

Before oneiric and chthonic mysteries comes the waking life on earth.

Before the moonlight world comes that of sunlight.

Walt Whitman did not lack for visions and myth but he began with leaves of grass.

The higher registers of phantasy and imagination flower from the natural economy of our creaturely fate and vicissitudes, and not in escape from them. Over against the hectic and febrile phantasms of de Quincy, prompted by opium, compare the ranges of sensitivity of a Gerard Manley Hopkins, nourished by human sympathies. How the dimensions of the mythological, the irrational, and the "Mothers" of the depths can best be construed in the modern world has its great prototype in the humanist Goethe.

Those who today seek the exotic and the occult make the plea that they find all else both insipid and confining. The traditional pieties of the family of man related from the beginning to toil, hearth, and community lack savor and are authoritarian. The celebrations and fables and poetries associated with the human creature and his life in the sun, rooted in his natural vitalities and the ultimate mystery of his being: all these they think to by-pass by some direct access to reality or to that which is beyond or before reality.

It is true that custom and error have often made our world unmiraculous and our social arrangements repressive. But the original freshness and liberty are not to be sought outside of the common endowments and limitations. Some of our contemporary rebels are in the right line in this respect: those identified with the ecological mystique, the new primitivism, those who honor toil and craft. This kind of sobriety and modesty reflects the biblical view of the creation, the good earth, and our human necessities. Here also the new "cosmic consciousness" with its reawakening of the faculty of wonder is to be prized. This is a further aspect of the current attitude of "affection for the environment."

So far, finally, as the themes of this book are addressed to theology and the churches my plea resolves itself into a reminder of the true stature of the Christian outlook and witness. What ranges of confidence have been forfeited and how widely our assurances have been intimidated! The compass and amplitude of our experience have been widely dwarfed as is evident at the level of basic apperception and matters taken for granted. It is reflected in the impoverishment of our visionary powers. It is a question of retracted horizons and shrunken categories of expectation. We rule out hidden operations of the Spirit and the unpredictable.

To all such reduction in the scope and expectations of faith the Gospel has its warning and promise. The scale of our measurement limits what we apprehend and receive. Therefore, "Take heed what you hear; the measure you give will be the measure you get, and still more will be given you" (Mark 4:21). "What we hear," or "how we hear" (Luke 8:18), point both to the unnecessary limitations of our awareness imposed by the "world" and to our proper responses to a dynamic and miraculous reality.

In my first chapter I observed that the church today needs to be reminded of the dimension of glory which is so central to the charters of its faith. What is intended here is in one respect a renewal of the religious imagination. But it is also a particular vision of the human lot. Nor is it only a question of elevation of view or transcendence as in the older phrase about seeing the world in the light of eternity. It is a question rather of heightened sensitivity for which the ordinary transactions of life are shot through with meaning, with moving charities, and with providence.

If one turns, for example, to the Gospels a modern reader can find them a baffling compound of realistic elements, incredible episodes, and mythical categories. This whole theater of persons, actions, and beliefs appears preternatural and hyperbolic. But, again, it is a question as to our estimate of mundane affairs. If our assumptions about the world are dwarfed and routinized then our measure of events either today or in the past are thus blinded. Granted a more sensitive, awesome, and magnanimous vision of mortals and their fates, then such a portrayal as is found in the Gospels would be in order. Miracles and myths would be in the nature of the case, however varying and particular might be their representation.

The Christian imagination, a theopoesis, is necessary in any time to safeguard this stature and these dimensions of reality. In their light the world today and our own theaters of action can, as in the beginning, be malleable to the Spirit.